ENCOUNTERS
DE LA SALLE AT PARMENIE

John Baptist de La Salle at prayer in the Parmenie chapel. A nineteenth century painting by Pellegrini hung on the wall of the restored chapel.

ENCOUNTERS
DE LA SALLE AT PARMENIE

LEO BURKHARD, F.S.C. & LUKE SALM, F.S.C.

Christian Brothers National Office
Romeoville, Illinois 60441-1896

Encounters: De La Salle at Parmenie
Copyright 1983 by Christian Brothers Conference
Romeoville, Illinois 60441-1896

Printed by Saint Mary's Press
Winona, Minnesota 55987

CONTENTS

ILLUSTRATIONS

FOREWORD

This volume is another in the series of translations of works heretofore unavailable in English that pertain to the life and work of Saint John Baptist de La Salle. The series was begun under the direction of the late Brother Charles Henry, F.S.C., former Superior General of the Institute of the Brothers of the Christian Schools.

The present volume follows the style and format of the earlier work in this series entitled *Beginnings: De La Salle and his Brothers.* Following as it does upon *Beginnings,* this little book might have been entitled *Endings.* However, as the reader will discover, the events at Parmenie turned out to be penultimate in the life and career of John Baptist de La Salle. The end came in the motherhouse at Saint Yon in Rouen where the Founder died in 1719, five years after he left Parmenie to resume the direction of his Institute.

Since the publication of the earlier volume, this writer has had the opportunity to visit, on three successive occasions, the places throughout France that featured so largely in the early history of the Institute: Reims, Laon, Paris and Rouen in the North; Avignon, Grenoble and Parmenie itself toward the South; Marseille, as far south as you can get in France, the Sainte Baume nearby, and the country to the West as far as Mende. These Lasallian "pilgrimages" have helped immeasurably in giving a sense of place and distance to the translator and, one hopes, a sense of authenticity to the translation and the supplementary material.

One striking feature of these journeys through France was the discovery that the Brothers still have active communities in so many of the places that witnessed the birth and early expansion of the Institute: not only in Reims, Paris, Rouen, Avignon and Marseille, but also in places less well known to American tourists such as Saint Denis, Laon, Troyes, Dijon and Mende. Although the seventeenth century school buildings have in most cases disappeared, the site is usually known, the parish church still survives, and so does a community of Brothers active in the educational apostolate.

Parmenie, the special focus of this study, is the name given to the property that crowns an imposing hill rising high above the valley of the Isere river, not far from Grenoble in southeastern France. It is the purpose of this volume to provide for an English speaking audience an introduction to the history of Parmenie and its significance for the life journey of John Baptist de La Salle and the Institute of Brothers that he founded. There has been a renewed interest in this place ever since the property was acquired by the Brothers in 1964. In the intervening years the ancient buildings have been restored, residence facilities expanded (though not as much as one would wish), and modern conveniences installed.

The work of restoration is due to the initiative, imagination, and plain hard labor of Brother Leo Burkhard, F.S.C. An American Brother from the Brothers' Province of New Orleans/Santa Fe, Brother Leo first came to Parmenie under circumstances that he relates in his introduction. In the process of obtaining the degree of Doctor in Letters from the University of Grenoble, Brother Leo wrote his dissertation on the history of Parmenie with special reference to the events there that involved John Baptist de La Salle. Afterwards he published in French a popularized version of his research entitled simply *Parménie*. It is this French popularization, in part translated and in part summarized and edited, that provides the framework and a good part of the text of the present volume. To this, a considerable amount of supplementary material has been added by Brother Luke Salm, F.S.C. in order to provide greater detail on the persons and events covered in the text. The introduction to each chapter identifies the material that is a translation of the Burkhard book and the supplementary material added by Salm.

In the process of translation some decisions had to be made with regard to a suitable English style. The French spelling of proper names has for the most part been preserved in transliterated form, with the exception of the Founder's given name. French ecclesiastical titles such as *Abbé, Monsieur, Monseigneur, Frère, Soeur* and the like are either translated or anglicized since their transliterated equivalents often mean something very different from the French. Except for direct quotations and citations in italics, French accents have been consistently omitted so as not to encumber the English text.

In view of the audience to which this book is addressed, it seemed advisable to eliminate footnotes altogether. Already reduced to a minimum in Burkhard's original popularization, most of the citations there are to sources in the French language not readily available to the English speaking reader. For the research oriented reader who might want to pursue the subject matter in greater depth, a brief introduction to each chapter indicates the principal sources on which the material in that chapter depends.

Finally, expressions of gratitude are due to those whose encouragement and assistance have made the production of this modest volume possible: first of all, to Brother Charles Henry, former Superior General, for inaugurating this series and for his continuing encouragement; to Brother Augustine Loes for a very critical reading of the manuscript and valuable suggestions for its improvement; to Brother Hilary Gilmartin and his associates at the Christian Brothers' Center in Romeoville, Illinois, for keeping the series alive and for their exacting supervision of the production process; to Brother Leo Burkhard for hospitality and fraternal sharing at Parmenie and, above all, for permission to publish this version of his experience and research; and then to all the Brothers in the communities in Paris, Reims, Rouen, Laon, Troyes, Dijon, Lyon, St. Etienne, Sauges, Mende, Avignon and Marseille for extraordinary hospitality and fraternal solicitude for this Lasallian pilgrim from an alien shore.

Luke Salm, F.S.C.
September 14, 1982
Feast of the Holy Cross

INTRODUCTION

My Encounter with Parmenie

This very personal introduction to the French original was translated by the author himself, Leo Burkhard, F.S.C.

There is always something mysterious about mountains. As far back as written history relates they have played an important part in our human earth while existence either as instruments of fear or messengers of peace, like Sinai and Fuji-Yama or Popocatepetl and Vesuvius. There is, I think, not a country in the world that cannot boast of its "eternal hills" with their mystery and their religion, their adventure and their intrigue, their enchantment and their terror.

I recall exploring, as a lad, and not without a certain apprehension, the famous Black Mesa which rises abruptly out of the volcanic ruins of central New Mexico. Here each day in a hidden cave, so the tale goes, a dreadful ogre devoured the bodies of six or eight youths kidnapped the previous night from nearby pueblos. Much further on to the South, in Old Mexico, I climbed one of the imposing pyramids of Teotihuacan and, from the very spot where centuries earlier human sacrifices were offered, I beheld, quite overcome by its imposing beauty, the extraordinary snow-capped Popocatepetl, the Indian's deity.

But it is to Dauphiny in France that I want to take you for the moment to discover another mountain, hardly large enough to merit the name, but rich nevertheless like no other in history and folklore, to Parmenie, a site of varied inspiration which has lost nothing of its centuries old enchantment. I first went there in the spring of 1957 having arrived in France the previous autumn. I was at the time winding up a Lasallian pilgrimage that had already taken me from the Pas de Calais to the old port of Marseille always in the footsteps of John Baptist de La Salle. As I climbed the steep grassy slope of Parmenie's southern flank, it was De La Salle's sojourn on this very mountain that occupied my thoughts and intrigued me to no end. In the long story I am about to tell, his place will not be the least conspicuous.

Then there was that shepherdess, popularly known as Sister Louise, who had become identified, as it were, with this silent mountain retreat and whose role in De La Salle's career had been decisive. I would delve into all that anew, here on the very spot where those interviews took place, and watch them re-enacted as it were, in imagination.

The narrow rocky path led on zig-zag past a small flock of sheep clinging, I thought impossibly, onto that steep slope, then lost itself in the trees and shrubbery hiding the summit. A little further along the way, a pleasant spring bubbled its message crystal clear to the silent woods. From the spring to the crest, I think I have never to this day listened to a more eloquent silence. The world lingered just far enough below to remain unheard, though doubtless still aflutter within the tiny hamlets spotting the valley of the Isere and the Bievre plains; the giant Alps rose already too distant to dwarf tiny Parmenie, and the precipices of the Vercors served efficiently to sever every remnant of Grenoble's disturbing civilization beyond the valley.

Coming out into the clearing at the summit, I stood spellbound for a few moments. No Roman fortifications, no medieval castle as I had expected, no signs of a glorious past now interred, perhaps forever. Ruins there were of a miniature chapel and monastery, ruins that spoke of war and the desolation that follows. I thought for a moment that I saw Lieutenant Claude Dulac de Montisambert disappearing beyond the crumbling remains into the monastery garden, tired of his military exploits. He too would figure in the story to be told.

To the left, opposite the chapel, on an elevated spot, the charred remains of a huge cross. In my imagination I associated it with the corsses I had seen burnt as a child by the fierce and mysterious Ku Klux Klan in America. What had taken place here? I would look into that, certainly, and write the details of a far more fantastic story than the escapades of the Klan, for Parmenie had once been the site of blasphemous rituals presided over by a new prophet Elias and attended by thousands of credulous country folk from far and near.

Climbing over the crumbling walls of the outer monastery and on into the abandoned chapel, I was overcome by the feeling of some strange presence. Was it that of the humble virgin Beatrice whose altar monument lay shattered at my feet, one slab still jealously clinging to her initials, engraven on it in large gothic letters: B. B. (Blessed Beatrice)? Or was it that other virgin who, I thought, stared down, desolate, from an empty niche above the rock altar, that Pieta I had discovered, lonely, in the church at the foot of the mountain, while all the villagers of Beaucroissant made merry at the fair.

There was, of course, that fair, one of the oldest in old, old France whose story was also to be told, for the virgin who had lived for centuries in her mountain resort of Parmenie had first brought the pilgrims here, though now there remained nothing but the fair. I somehow understood her reluctance to stay on in that hollow, profaned by inscriptions of every kind, and I could read in her sorrowful eyes as though she were present still, the grief that was hers at contemplating the havoc of this scene.

In the center of the chapel and partly covered by the debris of a crumbling partition, I spotted a large stone slab with an imbedded iron ring, but was quite unable to raise it, even slightly. What mysteries did it enclose? Would it fall to my lot to liberate the villainous Baunin who, as the peasants of the region related, had been trapped there for centuries in punishment for having amassed fabulous treasure, looting church and castle alike from Vienne to Grenoble?

Treasure seekers before me had been at work. The cloister, the gardens, the very cemetery itself had been violated. One tomb in particular caught my attention. It had been dug in the slope, with evident care. Though vandals, young or old, had broken it open and left the poor dead remains unearthed and restless, it had a story to tell of one named Sister Rosalie. She would tell it herself, a strange tale of a discovery she made on Parmenie. It would figure here with that of Sister Louise and Blessed Beatrice and the Pieta, with that of De La Salle and Claude Dulac, of Baunin the grave robber, of the false prophets Marion and Dubia (Elias) and their mistress Saint Nanon, and of the Beaucroissant fair which today remains as the sole testimony to the past grandeur of this tiny mountain of Dauphiny.

Leo Burkhard, F.S.C.

The hill of Parmenie as seen from the Isere Valley not far from Grenoble.

PROLOGUE

The Early History of Parmenie

This prologue is a summary of the historical material in the first four chapters of Leo Burkhard's Parménie. *The summary was prepared by Luke Salm; it has been reviewed and approved by the author.*

In Roman times, the hill of Parmenie occupied a commanding position overlooking the principal Roman road that led from Vienne to Grenoble which, before it became "Gratian's City," was known as Cularo. The name Parmenie comes from the Latin *para moenia* (alongside the walls) and indicates that the place was heavily fortified. There is also evidence of a shrine to Mercury and some indication that the worship of Isis may have been popular on a site where Druids had gathered for their strange rites centuries earlier. A deep cistern near the present chapel building still survives as a souvenir of the Roman days.

In the early Middle Ages, Parmenie served as a refuge for the earliest Christian bishops. Originally the entire area formed part of the diocese of Vienne. The bishops built a fortified priory there as a convenient and protected retreat from their political and military enemies. Later on, when the diocese of Grenoble was formed, it served the bishops of the new diocese in the same capacity against the attacks of the Saracens. It is believed that relics of the Holy Cross were kept here during these Saracen invasions. Parmenie thus became an important place of pilgrimage as early as the eighth century.

In Grenoble, September 14, the feast of the Exaltation of the Holy Cross, has always been a popular feast. The first church in Grenoble bore the title of the Holy Cross, probably to commemorate the return of the true cross to Jerusalem in the year 630. On September 14, 1219, shortly after midnight, a dam broke and the devastating flood that followed destroyed most of the city of Grenoble as it was preparing for the feast. A year later, the bishop of Grenoble led a pilgrimage to Parmenie to give thanks for those who had been spared. In time this annual pilgrimage spread out into the neighboring village of Beaucroissant (Blessed Crossing) and so developed into the annual September fair for which the village is still famous.

Up until 1257 the Augustinians had been in charge of the priory at Parmenie. In that year, Bishop Falque of Grenoble gave it over to the Carthusian nuns. The most famous of these was Blessed Beatrice d'Ornacieu. She was a visionary and a mystic. Her self-inflicted stigmata gave witness to her extraordinary devotion to the passion of Christ and stories continue to circulate about her unusual miraculous gifts. Eventually she became the prioress of a new Carthusian foundation at Eymeu. Shortly after her death the new monastery had to be closed. Her remains and those of her two companions were returned to Parmenie where they may still be venerated to this day.

During the fourteenth century the Carthusian nuns had great difficulty in maintaining the monastery at Parmenie itself. Lack of revenue and basic necessities led to the transfer of many of the nuns to more solidly established monasteries and to the sale of the property at Eymeu. Substantial gifts from the Avignon pope, Clement VII, helped to postpone the inevitable for a while. However, in the 1390's, the marauding bands of Raymond of Turrene began to ravage the countryside nearby. The nuns were forced to flee and Parmenie was put to the torch. When it became clear that the nuns would not return, the property reverted to the Bishop of Grenoble. It eventually became the common property of the town of Tullins and remained in ruins for two-hundred years until the advent of Sister Louise.

CHAPTER I

Sister Louise Comes to Parmenie

This chapter is a translation by Luke Salm of Chapter V of Leo Burkhard's
Parménie. *The translation follows the original except for the omission of a long
quotation describing Louise's successful search for the relics of Blessed Beatrice
d'Ornacieu.*

*The principal source for the material in this chapter is the anonymous
manuscript mentioned in the text and preserved in the archives of the diocese of
Grenoble. Burkhard also cites the subsequent biographies of Gras du Villard,*
Histoire de la Pieuse Bergère du Mont Parménie *(Grenoble: André Arnaud,
1752); and Dom Theodore Bellanger,* Soeur Louise, la Pieuse Bergère de
Parménie *(Paris: A. Levesque, 1863).*

The most extraordinary and engaging chapter in the history of the
high hill known as Parmenie involves the life of a humble shepherdess.
Her name was Louise Hours but she was known familiarly as "Sister
Louise."

In feudal times it had been Beatrice d'Ornacieu who abdicated her
high rank, left her ancestral castle and fled to the cloister of Parmenie to
practice voluntary poverty. Three hundred years later, in the fabulous
reign of King Louis XIV, it was Louise, a child of the people, a penniless
shepherd girl, who devoted her life to this sanctuary. She made the ruins
of Parmenie speak with a voice so powerful that it was heard even as far
away as the royal court.

There is no attempt here to authenticate the reputation for sanctity
that Louise, as did Beatrice, left behind in her native province of
Dauphiny. The purpose, rather, is simply to tell the story of how this
unusual peasant girl was able, almost miraculously, to restore the
ancient chapel of Parmenie that had been left in a state of total collapse
ever since the fifteenth century.

The most important source for what we know of Louise Hours is an

The Hermitage at Parmenie as it is today.

anonymous manuscript written shortly after her death in 1727. Years later, in the nineteenth century, Canon Auvergne, the secretary general of the diocese of Grenoble, published it in installments in *La Semaine Religieuse*. In 1877 he had it published as a separate brochure. Canon Auvergne attributed the original text to Berson de Ponceau, one of the directors of the retreat house at Parmenie after the death of Sister Louise. The present account follows this document rather closely.

Louise was born in 1646 in the parish of Touvet in the valley of the Gresivaudan, about fifteen miles from Grenoble. Her father was Benedict Hours, a native of Hauterives; her mother, Isabeau or Elizabeth Pelu, was originally from Voiron. Louise's father was employed as a forest ranger in the service of the Count of Ferrieres, while her mother worked as a domestic servant in the Count's castle. Louise was only two years old when her parents moved to a spot near the foot of the Parmenie hill in the parish of Beaucroissant. There they continued to be employed in various services for the Count of Ferrieres, whose castle known as Alivet was not far away. The Hours family received from the Count a small plot near the parish of Renage where they built as best they could a modest dwelling which later became known as "Little Parmenie." It was there that Louise grew up, in the shadow of the Parmenie hill, watching over her flocks in the fields and on the neighboring hillsides.

When she was fourteen years old, Louise was hired as a serving girl in the house of a merchant of Rives. There was also a priest living in the house at that time and Louise asked him to be good enough to give her some religious instruction. But within two years her father died and Louise had to return home to help her aging mother. She became a shepherdess once again, returning to the pastures of Parmenie which was always her favorite spot. She loved to wander among the scattered ruins of the ancient monastery of the Chartreuse nuns and to pray before Mary's altar which was still partially standing.

It was then, according to Gras du Villard, that "she began to conceive the great desire to have God worshipped once again in this place. For the moment it remained only a dream but it became stronger and stronger in a most extraordinary way every time she came up to the mountain."

Meanwhile, the better to provide for her mother's need for ready money, she was compelled to return to Grenoble to work again as a serving girl. After a few months she was called back to the bedside of her mother, who died shortly thereafter. This gave her the freedom to become more preoccupied with the direction her own life ought to take.

Louise was now able to spend more time on her beloved hilltop. One day—it was the feast of the Holy Cross in September—she left her flocks in the care of some of the other shepherd girls to go once more to visit the ruins of the chapel. While she was there, she thought she heard an interior voice saying over and over gain, "Here is the place that I have chosen to be worshipped; I want you to build here a shrine in my honor."

This occasioned a great deal of perplexity for Louise. She knew full well the enormous difficulties involved in accomplishing what she believed she had been commanded to do. On the other hand, she could not bring herself to disobey a direct command from God. One of her biographers writes: "For Louise, it was never a question of a vision or an apparition, neither was it a dream of her childish imagination. The voice that spoke to her was one of those powerful interior movements that captivate and fascinate us . . . Louise was never an ecstatic, a visionary, or given to such extravagances." For all that, however, she was accused of strange behavior and self-deception. Her own companions heaped abuse and ridicule upon her, rumors began to circulate about her, and she was reviled for acting like a visionary.

Quite naturally, Louise confided to her spiritual director her most intimate thoughts, especially the idea that dominated her, namely, to rebuild the ancient chapel of Parmenie in honor of the Virgin Mary. Her director at that time was Father Durand, pastor of the church at Voreppe. He was a straight-forward and sensible priest, advising her to practice humility and to guard against illusion. Louise began to speak of her great project to persons she thought might be able to help. Among them was Mother Bon, an Ursuline nun of Saint Marcellin, who had a reputation for holiness. She in turn brought the matter to Father De Gorges, a Dominican priest of Grenoble, well thought of for his virtue and religious insight. Father De Gorges, after thinking about it for a while, sent Louise to see the chancellor of the diocese, Father Claude Canel, canon and theologian of the church of Saint Andre and a counsellor to the Parliament. Only one step more was needed to bring Louise before the bishop himself.

All of this took place sometime in 1673 when Etienne Le Camus II was in his second year as Bishop of Grenoble. For some years before that he had followed his natural inclinations and tasted all the delights of the court of Louis XIV. But since then he had become a model for the clergy of France by reason of his zeal, his learning and his penitential life. He eventually merited elevation to the cardinalate; as Cardinal of Grenoble he became one of the most distinguished members of the Sacred College. To expect to appear before such a distinguished prelate was indeed a presumptuous undertaking for a poor shepherd girl like Louise who could neither read nor write and who spoke only the rude patois of her native village. She began by formally requesting Father Lyons, the bishop's chaplain and secretary, to arrange an interview for her with the bishop. But no sooner did Father Lyons hear her speak about an extraordinary inspiration to build a church than he wrote her off as a deluded visionary and, taking her by the arm, escorted her out of the room.

Humiliated but resigned, Louise went back to Father Canel who agreed to plead her case. Through his intervention Louise was at last granted an audience with the bishop who listened sympathetically to what she had to say. After a long period of waiting, the authorization finally came through for her to rebuild the shrine at Parmenie and to solicit the necessary funds.

In the full flush of her enthusiasm, Louise lost no time in getting started. She began to look for support in the nearby town of Tullins since that was the most populous parish in the area. At first she received nothing but misunderstanding. She was rebuffed and sent away as if she were crazy. The Count of Tonnerre, who was the overlord of Tullins, heaped the most humiliating insults upon her. He even set his dogs on her to chase her away.

Divine providence soon came to her aid, however. Another young girl, as poor as Louise, volunteered to accomapny her and to help her raise money. In Tullins, between the two of them, they collected less than 100 sous from a town that numbered between three and four thousand persons. Without letting themselves be discouraged by such small success, the two girls continued their fund raising in the Cote Saint Andre and at Saint Marcellin. Although the returns were not considerable, it was possible for Louise to begin the work of reconstruction on April 4, 1673. Almost to a man, the peasants of the countryside came to help her. Some provided the wood; others, despite the lack of access roads, arranged to transport the building materials free of charge; still others brought food for the workers, many of whom refused to accept pay for their work.

The funds from the first campaign were soon exhausted and Louise was forced to begin another. This time she went to Grenoble and managed to collect about 30 livres (the equivalent of about 300 U.S.A. dollars). By August 25, 1673 the walls had begun to rise again on the foundations of the ancient church. When the money began to run out once again, Louise undertook another fund raising expedition, this time in Valence. It went very well. In addition to almost 120 livres in silver, she came back with a donkey laden with all sorts of supplies including some rudimentary furniture and decorations for the chapel.

Upon her return from Valence, Louise found an agreeable surprise. All the tiles necessary to cover the chapel roof had been brought there in her absence, the gift of a charitable matron who lived nearby. Louise began at once to complete the vault and the roofing. Then came the work of finishing the interior. A large wooden railing was used to close off the entrance as a way of separating the sanctuary from the nave which had yet to be built.

Thanks to the energy that Louise brought to the work, the building was completed in less than a year, furnished and otherwise provided with everything necessary to have Mass celebrated there. When the preparations were finally complete, Louise had the consolation of seeing the chapel blessed by Father Canel, acting with the formal approval of Bishop Camus. The date was May 3, 1674. In order to link the chapel to its ancient past, Louise undertook a search for the remains of Beatrice d'Ornacieu, the saintly Chartreuse nun who had died in 1303, and her two companions. The search was successful and again, with the approval of the bishop, the relics were reinterred in a special niche built into the chapel wall.

So it was that the ancient chapel of Parmenie arose from its ruins. But Louise did not as yet know in what way God would be glorified by what she had undertaken. The enterprise had apparently been divinely inspired and visibly supported by divine help. While waiting for God's will to become more clearly manifest, Louise resolved to remain in this place, far from the world, to devote herself to her own sanctification and to act as a guardian for the chapel, dividing her time between prayer and manual work.

For this purpose, and in order to protect herself against the wolves that roamed the area and the violent winds that swept through this solitary place, she built adjacent to the chapel a small hut made of sticks and dried mud which she covered with a straw roof. In doing so, she seemed neither to provide for nor care about the lack of even ordinary comforts. According to Father Soland, the spiritual director at the time of Louise's death in 1727, this hut was still standing twenty years later.

After the blessing of the chapel and the departure of the pilgrims, Louise and her companion settled down in their little hut. They lived there for seven years, barely surviving on a diet that consisted for the most part of black bread and water. More often than not, their bread consisted of the leftovers given them by the shepherd girls of the neighborhood. Since they had to get their water from the spring at the bottom of the steep hill, it often happened that they had to do without it altogether. They had no chimney and so they could not light a fire, even in the most extreme cold, without either suffocating from the smoke or running the risk of having their thatched roof go up in flames.

Every once in a while, a priest would come the long distance to Parmenie to say Mass. But this happened very rarely. Most of the time, the two solitaries had to go down to the valley in all kinds of weather to assist at the daily Mass.

Isolated in the wilderness, Louise's modest chapel was like a gemstone waiting to be cut and polished. In time she saw the need for some new and important improvements. For one thing, all of the ancient monastery buildings were still in ruins and there was not a single habitable room. Father Canel, who from time to time came from Grenoble to visit Parmenie, decided that Louise should resume her fund raising in order to rebuild the living quarters. She again directed the work herself with the same zeal and good nature as before. When her financial resources gave out, she would go back again to her efforts to raise money, especially in Lyon, and each time she had more and more success. Thus within six months she brought to completion not only a considerable enlargement of the chapel building but also the erection of a residence large enough to house a priest and several retreatants as well as her companion and herself. The new chapel was much more impressive than the old, which was now used as a sacristy. Together the two parts measured more than thirty feet in length and sixteen feet in height.

In 1681, once the new construction was completed, Louise decided to see what she could do to get Bishop Le Camus to appoint a permanent chaplain for Parmenie. It could scarcely be expected that such a cautious and farseeing prelate would agree all at once without giving the matter long and serious study. Yet in order not to offend Sister Louise, he invited her to look herself for someone who would be both suitable for the post and willing to go to live there. No doubt the bishop thought that this solution would gain time and give him a respite from further importuning on the part of Sister Louise. After all, what priest would be willing to become a hermit in such a deserted place, generally lacking in every convenience? But much to the bishop's surprise, Louise came back only two days later accompanied by a holy priest of the diocese of Vienne whom she had selected for this good work.

The priest was the well known Father Roux, born about the year 1653 in La Frette, five miles or so from Parmenie. As soon as she left the audience with the bishop, Louise had gone on foot to seek out this very special priest. Father Roux let himself be convinced in spite of the objections and downright opposition of his associates. Roux was already fairly well known to the bishop from the recommendation of Father Canel who had spoken of him as a man most suited to undertake the ministry at Parmenie. Accordingly, after a lengthy interview, the bishop gave approval for Father Roux to preach and to administer the sacraments at Parmenie subject to the jurisdiction of the diocese. Father Roux settled down at Parmenie in October 1681 and for more than thirty years he worked there with extraordinary zeal.

Once Parmenie had its own spiritual director, the news spread rapidly throughout the entire province. It was said that the chaplain's simple and austere lifestyle was as extraordinary as that of Sister Louise herself. The good that was accomplished at Parmenie awakened in many people the desire to come there for retreats. But it was not possible at that period to accommodate them overnight. For that reason, Father Roux and Louise were advised to construct yet another building that could serve as a residence for women, while the earlier residence would be reserved for the men. Once the new building was completed, probably in 1686, Parmenie had two residence complexes, each of which could accommodate no fewer than eight retreatants. Soon even this proved to be inadequate and little by little additional rooms were added to the buildings.

On August 13, 1687, Bishop Le Camus came up the hill to Parmenie to preside over the formal sealing of the relics of Beatrice d'Ornacieu and her two companions. After a tour of the chapel and the cells of the retreatants, he was unable to conceal his admiration. Without hesitation, he gave permission to reserve the Blessed Sacrament day and night in the chapel tabernacle. He gave definitive authorization for the retreat exercises and himself outlined what he considered a suitable daily program. Retaining for himself, as all the previous bishops of Grenoble had done, the title of superior of Parmenie, the bishop appointed Father Roux as his vicar and conferred on him all the necessary ecclesiastical faculties.

The archives of the diocese of Grenoble still preserve the text of the decree issued on that occasion:

> Stephen Le Camus, by the divine sufferance and by the favor of the holy apostolic see, bishop and prince of Grenoble . . . We, having come up to the mountain of Parmenie in order to effect the sealing of the remains of Beatrice d'Ornacieu . . . We, having been edified more than we can say by the work that has been carried on in this solitude through the devotion of a poor shepherdess who has built there, with our consent and the aid of several charitable persons, a chapel dedicated to the Blessed Virgin under the title of Our Lady of the Crosses . . . We have installed there and do install by these presents, for as long a time as it will please us, the Reverend John Roux as our vicar with the title of Rector of the Chapel of Our Lady of the Crosses, and we grant him in consequence full jurisdiction over this house while reserving to Ourselves the immediate superiority . . . Given in Our holy house of Parmenie, the second day of September, 1687.

The retreats at Parmenie enjoyed considerable success. In the chapter that follows, attention will be given to two of the most distinguished among the retreatants: Saint John Baptist de La Salle, Founder of the Institute of the Brothers of the Christian Schools and Claude Francois Dulac de Montisambert, a former lieutenant in the Royal Regiment of Champagne.

For more than thirty years, Father Roux served as the director of the Parmenie retreats. These exercises brought together people of every rank and condition. The hill of Parmenie recovered its ancient reputation as a landmark. By the end of the seventeenth century it was considered to be one of the marvels of the Dauphiny country.

During all the time he served at Parmenie, Father Roux made the trip down from the hill only once. That was under doctor's orders in the hope of restoring him to health in the hospital at Voreppe. But the priest soon went back up to Parmenie where he died on June 8, 1712. His body was laid to rest in a small crypt which Sister Louise had dug out under the chapel floor and which Father Roux was the first to occupy.

The retreats were continued under the direction of Father Jean d'Yse de Saleon. It was through him that John Baptist de La Salle became acquainted with Parmenie. After Father De Saleon became himself a bishop, Louise went in search of a new chaplain. This she

25

found in the person of a Father Soland, the dean of the collegiate church of Montluel, a man noted for his unusual learning and great piety. Despite his advanced age, Louise predicted that he would continue as director at Parmenie for more than ten years and that she would die well before him.

She turned out to be right. Louise died at Parmenie on January 22, 1727 and Father Soland lived on until 1742. Louise was 82 years old when she died. She had spent fifty-four years on the mountain of Parmenie, living a life of austerity and penance, hard work, fatigue, poverty, contradiction and trials of every sort, above all in the exercise of a devoted charity that was for the most part unappreciated. In the last years she had given up all her administrative duties and she never again came down from her mountain retreat.

Shortly before her death, Louise had experienced an inflammation of the chest. She was tortured with a devouring thirst and such pressure in her lungs that she could scarcely breathe. On the morning of January 22, in the realization that she would not live to see the evening, she asked her companion to wash her hands and face, to give her fresh linen and to dress her as for a great feast day. Early in the afternoon she entered into her final agony. Toward evening she departed forever from her beloved Parmenie to undertake her journey to heaven.

Gras de Villard, one of her biographers writes: "The news of her death spread about very quickly. On the following day, despite the rigors of the winter season, there appeared on the snow-covered mountain of Parmenie such an enormous gathering of priests and the faithful that the obsequies had to be delayed in order to allow time to venerate the mortal remains of a woman whom people regarded as a saint."

The body of Sister Louise was laid to rest in the small crypt in the chapel of Parmenie alongside the remains of Father Roux.

CHAPTER II

Was Louise a Religious Sister?

The material in this chapter constitutes an appendix in the French original of Leo Burkhard. The translation is by Luke Salm.

In addition to the sources referred to in the previous chapter, the author cites several documents from the Grenoble archives; the Dictionnaire du Dauphiné *of Guy Allard (Grenoble: Allier, 1864); and a* Guide itinéraire *published by Mace in 1860 (the source of the quote that concludes the chapter).*

The title "Sister" given to the shepherdess of Parmenie has been the subject of much discussion. People who come to visit Parmenie often ask whether she was a member of a religious congregation of women, perhaps even a foundress. What follows is an attempt to summarize what can be said on the question.

Guy Allard, the first to mention Louise in a general history of the Dauphiny, does not give her the title "Sister." He writes:

> Permagne [sic!] had been a priory of the Augustinian order located on a mountain known as Saint Main . . . It has been in ruins now for more than a century, but during a period of several years a pious young girl named Louise David turned it into a devotional center. There was built for her a small house and eventually a chapel where other young women joined with her in devotional exercises. Together they served God under the supervision of a priest who acted as their spiritual director. There they brought up young girls in the fear of God, in simple manual skills appropriate to their condition, meanwhile teaching them how to read and write.

The author of this account is certainly misinformed. For one thing, he gives the name Louise David to Louise Hours. He is equally in error

Sister Louise. From an early eighteenth century painting.

when he says that young girls were reared and educated at Parmenie. Louise herself could neither read nor write and she spoke only the rough dialect of the region.

It is not known exactly when she began to be called Sister Louise. However, all of her biographers agree in speaking of her attraction to things religious despite her almost complete ignorance of the doctrinal content of her religious faith. After her father died, she was under continual pressure to get married so as to provide better for her mother and to make secure their few possessions. She always replied: "No, I do not wish to marry and if an engagement is forced upon me, I shall go so far away that you will never see me again." Sometimes she would say in jest to her female companions, "I would like to build a convent for young girls where we could all work together in the service of the good Lord."

Louise was employed for a time in Grenoble as a serving girl in the home of a very religious widow who promised to get her accepted as a Sister in the Convent of Saint Claire. But after three months in the employ of this widow, divine Providence called Louise back to the bedside of her mother who had fallen seriously ill. After her mother's death people began once again to urge Louise to marry. They even went so far as to introduce her to a young and upright stonemason who was well thought of among the people. Louise replied that before they could consider marriage they would first have to separate from each other, that they should pray and receive the sacraments frequently during this time to discover the will of God. Some time later the two of them met again but only after it had become clear that Louise was determined to preserve her freedom and that there was no further possibility of marriage between them.

Once she made this decision, Louise gave herself over more and more to a life of prayer. Her earliest biographer states that "it was in the secret encounters alone with God on Mount Parmenie that she was inspired to consecrate herself entirely to God by a vow of virginity. This she did with the approval of her confessor and with a genuine determination to observe it scrupulously." The author of another anonymous biography suggests that in his opinion she made the three vows of religion—poverty, chastity and obedience—without saying anything to anyone. It was only later, he says, that she would have revealed this secret to Father Canel, her spiritual director. In any case, she had already and for a considerable time renounced any sort of ornament in her dress, retaining only the plain black costume of a

29

shepherdess to which she then added a plain white covering for her head.

In a sense, then, it could be said that from 1670 on, that is, three years before she began her entreaties with Bishop Le Camus in an effort to get his approval to rebuild the chapel at Parmenie, Louise Hours had already become "Sister Louise." She was leading a life that was deeply religious without, however, being constrained by either monastic enclosure or the specific apostolic work that membership in some congregation might have assigned her to do. Under the direction of Father Canel, she was able to preserve a certain liberty of action that was necessary if she were to bring to a successful completion the mission that Providence seems to have confided to her.

A somewhat different question is whether or not Louise herself could be considered the foundress of a new religious congregation. Guy Allard seems to point in that direction. This gets some support from the fact that there is mention of a group of women at Parmenie called "Sisters" over a period of time that covers nearly two centuries.

> A young girl from Renage named Louise, the daughter of the falconer Benoit Hours, a girl who possesses no temporal goods but who is rich in virtue, asked permission of the bishop to rebuild the chapel, to raise funds for this purpose and to take up residence on the site . . . This girl, together with two other young women, has lived there for ten years in a wooden hut adjoining the chapel which she built herself . . . The bishop visited this hut where the three young women live. It is very small with room only for themselves and the few goats that they own. Louise maintains all the outward marks of her former occupation which was to shepherd flocks of goats. At first glance this young woman seems to be rather simpleminded. Yet her simplicity carries with it a great deal of sound judgment and that is one reason why she has succeeded so very well up until now. Furthermore, a deep religious spirit is evident in all that she does . . .
>
> Quite a number of young women have asked to join Sister Louise, but the bishop does not think that this is the time to increase the number at Parmenie. He has put Father Canel in charge of the chapel and has given him supervision of these young women whom he comes to visit from time to time. Sister Louise and her companions lead a common life

and they differ in no way from the other unmarried young women of the countryside, except that they give themselves much to prayer. They join to their ordinary manual work the exercises of piety that Father Canel prescribes for them. It is in no way clear what all of this will lead to since it will become increasingly difficult for these women to maintain themselves without a regular income and without monastic enclosure. However nothing has yet occurred in this enterprise except what is laudable. For that reason the bishop has not given any specific orders concerning them. For the moment he is content to encourage them in their work and their exercises of piety, penance and mortification. He has warned them not to use religious devotion as an excuse to become soft and lazy. After giving them a small alms, the bishop terminated his visit and returned to Grenoble.

After the death of Sister Louise, the other young women who were her companions continued to live at Parmenie. They were known as the "Domestic Sisters of the Retreat House of Our Lady of Parmenie." At least that is how they are described in the death certificates preserved in the Parmenie archives of the chancery office of the diocese of Grenoble. Sister Marie Martelon died on July 25, 1734 and Sister Dominique Sarra died on September 8, 1742. Both were buried in the small crypt under the chapel nave by Father Berson de Ponceau, the director of Parmenie at the time. Gras du Villard would add to this list the name of Sister Marie Dagot who had been assigned to the house of Parmenie by the bishop. She died on June 3, 1750 and was buried in the same crypt by Du Villard himself. Also buried in the chapel crypt was Marianne Dorey de Brosse, the widow of the notary Scipion Cochet. She died on May 14, 1755.

Canon Gras du Villard, who was the retreat director at Parmenie from 1750 to 1769, provides many details concerning the Sisters of Parmenie and the problems he had in dealing with them. Thus he says:

> The Sisters in the service of Parmenie have been established there mainly to be of service to persons of their own sex who come to this sanctuary to make a spiritual retreat. Under the direction of an ecclesiastical superior, they form a small community. Each day they go to the chapel for prayers, spiritual reading and other exercises of piety. In accordance with the will of Sister Louise, they possess jointly a share in

the movable and immovable goods which that pious woman left them as a legacy. They share the annual income from a capital fund of two thousand livres that enables them to continue their work. In case the Sisters of Parmenie should cease to exist, the two thousand livres would revert to the heirs of M. de Fusselet, their benefactor who left this money to them in his will.

For all that, it does not seem that these "Sisters" were religious women in the strict canonical sense. They would not have made vows. Furthermore, several documents attest to the marriage of one or another of them during the time that Father Gras du Villard was Director of Parmenie.

During the period of Parmenie's decline and the schism of Father Marion, that is to say, from the time of the French Revolution up until 1829, there was at Parmenie a woman called "Sister Therese" Thermos, but it is likely that she was little more than the mistress of Claude Dubia, the charlatan who called himself the prophet Elias.

Once that schism was over, there came to Parmenie a fine young woman from a nearby village. Her name was Caroline Rosalie Dupont and she was known to the people in the neighborhood as "Sister Rosalie." she died at Parmenie on May 23, 1873. The inscription on her tombstone reads: "Sister Rosalie, Servant of Our Lady of Parmenie." She seems to have been the last person at Parmenie to have been known by the title "Sister." She is still venerated in the area as a latter-day Sister Louise.

Thus Sister Louise seems to be the only one among all the domestic Sisters or "Servants of Our Lady of Parmenie" to have ever taken vows. Also, from 1708 on she was member of the Third Order of St. Dominic. Gras du Villard has preserved a copy of the act of her profession and testifies personally to its authenticity. It could be said, therefore, that Louise Hours did in fact have the right to be called "Sister," at least after 1708 by reason of her belonging to the Third Order of St. Dominic. On the other hand, it would be inaccurate to attribute to her the title of foundress of a religious congregation or any sort of a religious institute.

A third and final question is whether or not Sister Louise can be credited with inaugurating the retreat center at Parmenie. It would be more accurate to say that she was the instrument of divine Providence in restoring the lofty site where these retreats could take place. The retreat center itself was established by the initiative taken for his diocese by Cardinal Le Camus. The work was carried on and developed by Father Canel who was the superior at Parmenie, the confessor and spiritual director of Sister Louise.

Once again, Gras du Villard tells the story:

Here follows an account of the circumstances that led Cardinal Le Camus to grant the request of the pious shepherdess who had been inspired to rebuild the house at Parmenie.

This prelate had already acquired a strong spirit of penitence through his contacts with the Trappists under the Abbe de Rance. It was one of the cardinal's principal concerns to find a suitable place where he could provide for the training of candidates for the priesthood in an atmosphere of peace and recollection.

His first step was to take advantage of what divine Providence had already provided and so he arranged for the construction of a fine chapel and number of cells in a castle that belonged to the diocese known as the Castle of the Plain. This castle was only a mile or two from Grenoble and it was there that he sent the first seminarians. He himself went to live with them as their professor and spiritual director.

After a time, the cardinal thought that he could establish the seminary on a more solid basis by relocating it in the Abbey of St. Martin, which also was dependent on the diocese. For this purpose he undertook to enlarge the abbey. Work was already underway when he learned that the king had finally acceded to his request by ordering that a Protestant church, just opposite the episcopal palace in Grenoble, be closed. The cardinal bought the building for 20,000 francs and had it altered according to his plans. By 1678 it was in suitable condition for him to transfer the young seminarians from the Castle on the Plain to this new location. He then placed them under the direction of the Fathers of the Oratory.

Cardinal Le Camus then turned the Castle on the Plain into a retreat center for the priests of his diocese. He organized annual retreats, bringing the priests there by turns, feeding them at his own expense, and himself giving two conferences a day, each of which lasted over an hour. This continued until the cardinal's death which occurred on September 12, 1707.

It was during the period when arrangements for these two centers were going forward that God inspired the shepherdess we have already mentioned to come to the cardinal seeking his permission to rebuild the chapel and the other buildings that lay in ruins on the mount of Parmenie.

Cardinal Le Camus had himself been considering for some time the possibility of opening a third retreat center where lay people, and perhaps priests, might find it easy to go apart and think seriously about the state of their souls and their eternal salvation. Before giving permission to rebuild the house at Parmenie, the cardinal wanted to see the property for himself and to determine whether it would be suitable for such a purpose. Accordingly, in the course of his visitation of the parishes of his diocese, he made an inspection of the property on top of the hill.

Once he had been to Parmenie, the cardinal began to realize its possibilities. He noted the favorable location and what it was exactly that the shepherdess was trying to do. Soon thereafter he summoned Sister Louise to come to his residence. Recognizing at once that she was obviously moved by the Spirit of God, he gave his consent for her to undertake the restoration of the buildings. At the same time he appointed Father Canel, a canon of the church of St. Andre, to direct the project of this pious young woman. From then on she was always guided by the insights of that worthy priest. Helped by his advice and talent, as well as by the support of a great number of other devout persons, she was able to complete the reconstruction of the chapel and the house at Parmenie.

As soon as the buildings were in suitable condition, Father Canel formally blessed the chapel. From then on he organized a series of retreats which he personally directed under the supervision of Cardinal Le Camus. The cardinal himself drew up the original daily schedule for the retreats. Some time later, the cardinal appointed a priest named Father Roux to take over as director of the retreats, conferring on him the powers as penitentiary and grand vicar for the Parmenie house, to govern it under the immediate jurisdiction of the Bishop of Grenoble and his successors.

In conclusion it could be said that whatever the influence of Sister Louise might have been in relation to the Servants of Our Lady of Parmenie, whatever her role in setting up the retreat program, her true title to glory rests undiminished because of the person she was. As one author has remarked, "Whenever we encounter on a grand scale or on a small scale a life of such nobility, purity and devotion, we ought to respond with respect, tell the story simply without fictitious embellishments and offer it for admiration and perhaps even for imitation by others."

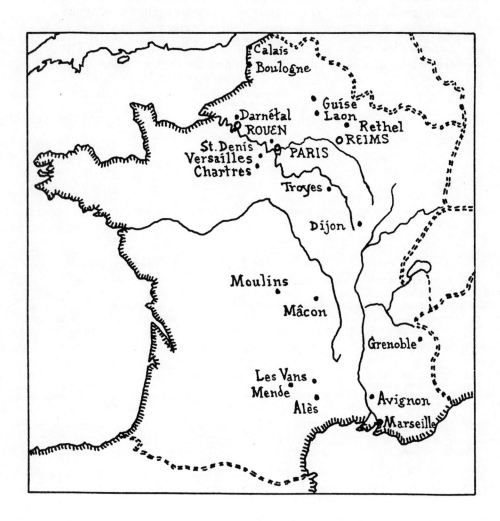

36

CHAPTER III

John Baptist de La Salle Comes to Parmenie

This chapter is a translation by Luke Salm of Chapter VI of Leo Burkhard's Parménie. *Additional material, several pages in length, has been interpolated into the translation to provide more detail on the sojourn of De La Salle in the south of France.*

The original biographers of De La Salle, Bernard, Blain and Maillefer, were all contemporaries of the Founder and knew him personally. Bernard was himself one of the Brothers. Blain was the ecclesiastical sponsor of the Brothers in Rouen during the last years of De La Salle's life. Dom Elie Maillefer was a nephew of the Founder. Bernard and Blain had at their disposal a number of documents from De La Salle himself as well as the written memoirs of the early Brothers. Blain especially likes to paraphrase or quote directly from these documents, most of which have since disappeared.

These early sources are not without their problems, however. The manuscript of Brother Bernard is incomplete and it was not deemed worthy of publication at the time it was written. The four volume biography of Canon Blain is heavily inflated with eighteenth century pietisms and other exaggerations aimed at advancing the cause of canonization. Maillefer, working independently and from memory most of the time, tends to gloss over painful or controversial situations. All three are imprecise as to names, places and dates and in general show little interest in the sort of documentation that characterizes contemporary scholarship.

In addition to the earliest biographies, both the French text of Burkhard and the interpolated material by Salm have been able to draw on more contemporary studies: Georges Rigault, Histoire Générale de l'Institut des Frères des Ecoles Chrétiennes, *Tome I (Paris: Plon, 1937); W. J. Battersby (Brother Clair Stanislaus, F.S.C.),* St. John Baptist de La Salle *(New York: Macmillan, 1957); and Yves Poutet, F.S.C.* Le XVIIe Siècle et les Origines Lasalliennes, *Tome II (Rennes: Reunies, 1970).*

During all the time that Sister Louise, under the inspiration of divine Providence, was occupied in the Dauphiny with the restoration of an ancient foundation, there was a young canon of the cathedral of Reims in the distant province of Champagne who was occupied with quite a different kind of foundation, one that was destined to have its fate decided at Parmenie. The canon was John Baptist de La Salle, the foundation was the Institute of the Brothers of the Christian Schools.

The encounter at Parmenie between Father De La Salle and Sister Louise in the year 1714 is perhaps the most important event that ever took place in that mountain retreat. It would seem that Sister Louise, guided by invisible forces, appeared on the stage of history at the precise moment when John Baptist de La Salle needed her. A whole series of circumstances, surely more than mere coincidences, gives reason to suppose that if this providential encounter between two holy people had not taken place, the work of De La Salle might have perished without a trace. Instead of spreading as it did throughout the whole world, De La Salle's vision would today be lost among the many legends associated with Parmenie.

The facts speak for themselves. Shortly after she had accomplished her divinely appointed mission with De La Salle, Sister Louise disappears from the scene. The house of Parmenie, which she without realizing it had providentially prepared for this extraordinary encounter, little by little fell back again into oblivion.

Louise was already five years old when John Baptist de La Salle was born in Reims on April 30, 1651. The De La Salles were people of quality, rather well off financially. In addition, John Baptist himself, from the time he was sixteen years old, had a considerable income from his position as a canon of the cathedral of Reims. When he had completed his preliminary studies in the university of his native city, he went to Paris in 1670 to continue his preparation for the priesthood there at the Seminary of Saint Sulpice. His association with Saint Sulpice was the reason that he became friendly later on with two priests from Grenoble, Claude Canel and Jean Yse de Saleon, who were to have such an important role in the events that involved De La Salle at Parmenie.

The circumstances that led De La Salle to make a series of decisions, resulting eventually in the establishment of the Institute of the Brothers of the Christian Schools, are every bit as providential as those that led Louise Hours to rebuild Parmenie. In a personal memoir written in 1690 on the origins of the Institute, De La Salle himself stated that God led him much further into the enterprise than he would otherwise have been willing to go: "God, who guides all things with wisdom and serenity and whose way it is not to force a person's inclinations, willed to commit me entirely to the work of the schools.

The good Lord did this in an imperceptible way and over a long period of time so that one commitment led to another in a way that I did not foresee at the beginning."

In order to devote himself entirely to this work, De La Salle resigned his post as canon. He distributed his personal wealth to the poor during the famine of 1684 which ravaged a large part of France. By these acts he effectively abandoned himself and his work entirely to divine Providence. From then on the work of the schools began to prosper: it had its first success at Reims, then spread to Paris and from there to all the provinces of France.

The first Brothers' school in Grenoble was opened in 1708. By that time, the shrine at Parmenie, restored a quarter of a century earlier by Sister Louise and Father Roux, had assumed a considerable importance in the Dauphiny country. There were, besides, two mutual friends of Father De La Salle and Sister Louise, namely Jean Yse de Saleon and Claude Canel, both of them canons of the collegiate church of Saint Andre in Grenoble. It had been at their request, in fact, that De La Salle had sent two of his Brothers to the Dauphiny province. Little did he think that within a short time a series of tragic events would lead him to the same province, to the hill of Parmenie, where the destiny of the young Institute would be decided.

By the same token, Sister Louise and Father Roux had themselves just barely survived a severe crisis. There was a new bishop in Grenoble, Alleman de Montmartin, who had indicated to them that as the result of some complaints he intended to close down the retreat center at Parmenie. Fortunately, Father Canel was able to intervene and save the situation. Then Father Roux died in 1712. The sanctuary at Parmenie and its retreat programs thus came under the direction of Father De Saleon who in this way became the instrument of divine Providence in the events of 1714 that involved John Baptist de La Salle.

In order to appreciate the significance of the encounters at Parmenie, it is necessary to recall the difficulties that De La Salle had encountered from the very beginning of his enterprise, a venture that was in so many respects a revolution in the educational field. From the very beginning, he was ridiculed in his native Reims. When the first school was opened in Paris in 1688 in the parish of Saint Sulpice, false accusations were made against him to the pastor, Father De La Barmondiere. The masters of the pay schools in Paris tried twice, in 1690 and again in 1698, to put an end to what they considered a dangerous movement.

The worst troubles began in 1696 when the new pastor of Saint Sulpice, Father De La Chetardye, tried to take charge and to govern the Brothers according to his own way of thinking. De La Salle well understood that this would endanger the whole future of his Institute and so he would not yield control over the Brothers and the school. From that time on De La Chetardye developed an intense hatred of De La Salle and used against him the powerful influence he had with Cardinal De Noailles, the Archbishop of Paris. It wasn't long before the cardinal notified De La Salle that he was to be relieved of all title to the superiorship and that another priest would be appointed to take charge of the community of the Brothers. The Brothers protested that nothing would ever separate the sons of De La Salle from their spiritual father and the cardinal had eventually to yield. To help restore calm, the Founder went in 1705 with his novices and some of the teaching Brothers to the remote suburb of Saint Antoine. But even there they had yet to endure a thousand misfortunes. A year later the enemies of De La Salle, in particular the teachers' guild of Paris, after obtaining writ after writ against him, won their case in the courts. Heavy fines were levied against De la Salle and the Brothers and all their school furnishings were confiscated.

The final and most terrible blow fell in 1712. Some years earlier, De La Salle was visited by a young cleric named Clement, the son of a famous Paris surgeon. Together, De La Salle and Clement founded a normal school for lay teachers in rural areas. Then suddenly and unexpectedly, the young Clement was given a rich benefice and a noble title. He lost all interest in the work of the school and refused to pay the sum of money he had agreed upon in a promissory note. Urged on by his father, he accused De La Salle of having suborned him as a minor and of forcing him to sign the promise of money. The Clement family brought the matter to court before the civil officer of the Chatelet of Paris. The intrigue against De La Salle was evident from the start. After a long period of litigation he eventually lost the case. The judgment against him was severe: he had to forfeit all that he himself had invested in the project and repay as well all that the young Clement had contributed. In a final insult, the formal sentence implies a challenge to his title as superior of the Brothers; he is designated "Monsieur De La Salle, priest and so-called Superior General of the Brothers of the Christian Schools of the city of Reims."

Even before the final judgment was handed down in the Clement affair, De La Salle had begun to turn his attention to the communities and schools that had been opened in the south of France. Since it was the events that occurred during the two visits to the South that eventually brought the Founder to Parmenie and caused him to remain there, it is appropriate to describe now in some detail the circumstances that gave rise to the profound discouragement that may have led De La Salle to consider, however tentatively, the possibility of giving up the work altogether.*

The first school to be opened in the South was in the papal city of Avignon. Despite the contradictions in the early biographers, it is now certain that this took place in 1703. A year earlier De La Salle had sent the two Drolin brothers, Brother Gabriel and Brother Gerard, to Rome to assure at least a token presence of the Institute in the Eternal City. Gerard Drolin soon became disillusioned with the prospects there. As he was returning to France with the intention of leaving the Institute, he stopped off at Avignon. There he lodged with Jean Pierre de Chateaublanc, the papal treasurer of the city and a man interested in establishing a school for the poor in Avignon. Gerard Drolin was able to act as an intermediary with De La Salle for the foundation of the Avignon school, his last act of service for the Institute.

The Founder was delighted at this development, especially in view of the troubled situation with the educational and ecclesiastical authorities in Paris. The Archbishop of Avignon at the time was Laurent Fieschi. He was resident in Paris since he was also serving as papal nuncio to France. Once the arrangements for the school in Avignon were complete, De La Salle wrote enthusiastically to Gabriel Drolin, still in Rome and alone there, about the Brothers who were leaving for Avignon to open the school: "I presented them to His Excellency, the Archbishop of Avignon, Extraordinary Nuncio to France. He received them cordially and gave them his blessing before they left, and he did so with great pleasure."

This blessing was important to De La Salle since Fieschi could not have been ignorant of the difficulties with the church authorities in Paris. The blessing of the nuncio implied more than local approval or approval only of these Brothers; it implied as well approval for the distinctive lifestyle and habit of the Brothers; it gave them a certain

---

*NOTE: The several pages that follow are not found in the text of Burkhard but are interpolated to provide more ample background for this important period in the life of De La Salle and his Institute.—BLS.

autonomy and opened up the possibility at least of direct contact with Rome.

When the Brothers finally arrived in Avignon they were well received by Antoine Banquieri, the Vice Legate. In a short time the school was so prosperous that larger quarters had to be provided. In 1705, De La Salle could write to Drolin: "The schools in Avignon are going well. We have four Brothers there and we are soon going to have a house that can accommodate as many as twenty." When the writing masters in Avignon arose in opposition to the Brothers, as they had in Paris, the powerful support of the Avignon authorities for the Brothers resulted in a favorable judgment: the Brothers were allowed to accept boys of all social classes into their gratuitous schools.

Eventually Fieschi was summoned to Rome and became a cardinal while Banquieri was named Governor of Rome. Both became powerful advocates for the Institute at the papal court. The favorable testimony of Archbishop De Gantery, who succeeded Fieschi in Avignon, had great weight in obtaining the Bull of Approbation for the Institute after the Founder's death.

It was out of Avignon that the first Brothers' school was founded in Marseille, a very different and much more tumultuous city. The parishes surrounding the old port were filled with wandering ragamuffins with nothing to do but watch the coming and going of the ships. The sailors themselves could neither read nor write; most of them had no religious training and many were attracted to the Moslem religion while others joined the roaming bands of pirates. Facing this situation, the town authorities, hearing of the success of the Brothers' school in Avignon, contacted De La Salle and obtained his approval to draw two Brothers from the Avignon community. Classes began in Marseille on March 6, 1706 in the port parish of Saint Laurent. The success was instantaneous: more than 200 pupils presented themselves on the second day. Before long, proposals were being drawn up to have the Brothers take over schools in all the important parishes of the city.

Avignon and Marseille are on a direct route along the Rhone river, south from Lyon and Paris. But there were other southern towns to the west that were also seeking to have the Brothers open schools for the poor. Farthest west and most important of these was Mende, the capital of the Gevaudan, more than 140 miles from the Rhone valley. The countryside between is very beautiful but difficult of passage, even today, with roads ascending and descending through canyons and gorges, up steep mountainsides and across rough plateaus. This whole area had been thoroughly infiltrated with Hugenot Protestants during the seventeenth century and served as a center for the resistance movement against the religious policies of Louis XIV. To support the King in his attempt to eliminate the Protestant religion from Catholic France, the local pastors in this region had special reasons for obtaining competent teachers to counteract the Protestant influence and to give a thorough and effective instruction in the doctrines of the Roman Catholic faith. Accordingly, Brothers' schools were opened in Ales in 1707, in Les Vans in 1711, as well as in Mende.

The school in Mende was opened in 1707 with the full support of Bishop De Piencourt who provided in his will for the continued support of the Brothers and guaranteed their independence. The agent for De La Salle was Brother Ponce who was acting out of Avignon as a sort of regional superior for all the Brothers in the South. Although De La Salle was anxious to have at least five Brothers in any one center to assure a viable community life, Brother Ponce began to teach the first class at Mende all by himself. When he fell ill after only a week or two, De La Salle sent two others to replace him. But the small size of the Mende community, its distance from the principal centers of the Institute, and the constant changes in its membership rendered this remote outpost a source of great concern for De La Salle.

While the Clement case was still pending back in Paris, De La Salle became convinced that his continued presence there would do more harm than good. Thinking that this might be the ideal time to see personally to the new foundations in the South, he left the capital in February, 1711. In the course of his journey he was able to visit the communities in Avignon, Marseille, Ales, Les Vans and Mende. The route from the Rhone river across to Mende, by way either of Ales or Les Vans, was particularly perilous, both by reason of the rugged terrain and the roving bands of outlawed Protestant Camisards, as they were called. When the Founder arrived at Mende for the first time he was thoroughly exhausted; the journey on foot was long and tiresome and his chronic rheumatism was giving him much pain. He paid his respects to the bishop and the civil authorities, hearing from them nothing but praise for the Brothers and glowing reports about their effectiveness in the school and their influence for good. He left Mende quietly for fear that he might be detained there overly long. By that time, he had learned that a judgment was imminent on the Clement affair and his presence was required once again in Paris.

De La Salle stayed in Paris throughout most of the winter of 1711-

1712. Part of the time he devoted to preparing a written deposition to explain the intent and meaning of certain documents that had been brought into the Clement case together with the correspondence between himself and the young Abbe. He then put the entire dossier in the hands of the lawyers. Early in the Lent of 1712, without waiting for the final judgment of the court, he departed Paris once again and headed for the South. This second journey was destined to be much longer in duration, more personally devastating to himself, and more decisive for his Institute.

It began encouragingly enough in Marseille. He was received cordially by Bishop Belsunce who, ever since he took over the see in 1709, had been negotiating with De La Salle to open a novitiate in his diocese. Plans were underway to have the Brothers take over the schools in the parishes of Saint Martin and Notre Dame des Accoules. For this purpose it would be necessary to have a suitable number of Brothers recruited from the Marseille area. The language, culture and lifestyle in Provence were so different from those of the North that it would be unrealistic to expect teachers from Reims, Rouen and Paris to be effective in such a different environment. It is not surprising then that the influential townspeople were generous in their support of the new novitiate project. When it opened in August or September 1712 many candidates presented themselves for admission to the Society.

De La Salle wrote to Gabriel Drolin that he hoped to send a Brother from the Marseille novitiate to join him in Rome; that there was good reason to hope that the Brothers would soon be in charge of schools in all four quarters of Marseille. De La Salle was himself preparing to leave for Rome when, in the act of saying goodbye to Bishop Belsunce, he was persuaded to stay to arrange for the opening of the school in the Accoules. He returned to the Brothers' community that he just left hours before and is reported to have said: "God be blessed! Here I am back from Rome."

But suddenly things changed. The school in the Accoules was never opened, the school proposed for the Brothers in the parish of Saint Martin was put in charge of a young seminarian, financial support for the novitiate dried up and postulants no longer presented themselves. A wholly new attitude toward De La Salle had developed in the course of the few months between September 1712 and March 1713. What had happened?

The biographers from Blain to Battersby have traditionally blamed the machinations of the Jansenist party for initiating a whispering campaign against De La Salle. More critical contemporary studies find this explanation too oversimplified. For one thing, the publication in France of the Bull *Unigenitus,* and the proscription of the "appellants" against the Bull to a General Council, was still a year away. The issue of Jansenism, although certainly in the air, was not that acute in the Marseille of 1712 and the early months of 1713. Additional reasons, then, are needed to explain the sudden change of attitude.

Part of the explanation may lie in the expectation of the prominent townspeople of Marseille. They may have been willing enough to support a novitiate to supply native teachers for their own schools in their own city. When they heard that De La Salle would consider the Marseille novices available for assignment elsewhere they began to withdraw their support. Also, the school board of Marseille was much under the influence of the catechetical center in Lyon where the policy, following the ideas of Charles Demia, was to have young priests and seminarians employed as catechists in the schools for the poor. Some seminarians had been so engaged in Marseille before the Brothers arrived there; it is altogether likely that these young ecclesiastics would have supported any movement to discredit the Brothers who replaced them. In fact, some of the legacies and foundations that were the source of support for the Brothers and their novitiate had specified that the monies be used to engage "ecclesiastics" for the teaching of the poor. Since De La Salle refused to have his Brothers receive the tonsure to fulfill this technicality, he was accused of obstinacy. Litttle by little the pastors of Saint Martin and the Accoules began to side with those who preferred the Lyon-Demia model that envisioned candidates for the priesthood as the ideal teachers for the schools. Although Bishop Belsunce made clear his personal preference for the Brothers, he had no legal control over the money that was made available for their support.

Another source of opposition to De La Salle was even more painful and embarrassing. The two Brothers who had been conducting the school in the parish of Saint Laurent for six years before the Founder arrived in Marseille had become accustomed during that time to a great deal of independence and freedom. Many of the obligations of the Common Rule and the practices of community life were impossible to maintain with only two together, such things as accusation of faults, advertisement of defects, community recreation, reading at meals and the like. In addition these Brothers had developed a strong following among the people of the parish.

When De La Salle insisted that these Brothers join the novitiate community and resume the regular routine of community life, they objected strenuously. They complained to the people of the parish that they were being taken away from the center of parish life, forced twice daily to make the long trek across town, and thus be less at the disposal of the parish that supported them. The parishioners sided with the two Brothers and made their representations to De La Salle. Again he would not yield, citing the central importance of regular community life for the Brothers. Again he was accused of intransigence. When news of the dispute reached Avignon, even Brother Ponce, who should have been more loyal to his chief, sided with the disgruntled Brothers against the Founder. The Brothers were increasingly heard to say: "Everything was going along fine until you came along. Why do you come here to destroy the whole enterprise rather than help to build it up?"

In the face of this opposition, De La Salle began to blame himself and decided once again that his continued presence was doing the Brothers more harm than good. Taking the pilgrim's staff, he quietly left Marseille and made his way over the thirty miles or so up to the Sainte Baume, the sacred grotto halfway up a vertical cliff where Mary Magdalen is said to have spent the last years of her life in repentance. Popes, kings and saints had made the pilgrimage before De La Salle and many have done so since. It was either there, in the hospice adjoining the grotto, or in the nearby monastery of Saint Maximin down on the plain, that the beleaguered Founder sought peace for his soul in prayer, fasting and solitude.

This pattern of withdrawal from the scene of controversy gave some credence to the rumors that began to circulate in Marseille that De La Salle was about to abandon the Brothers and leave the Institute to the designs of Providence and its own devices. Even Blain admits that there was some element of truth in this: the Founder, he says, had indeed thought from time to time that he might someday retire to a remote parish and there work for the conversion of hardened sinners. But, as Blain also remarks, these musings never came to anything in practice. Insofar as they were perceived as having any foundation, these rumors may have strengthened the resolve of those Brothers who earnestly wanted to keep De La Salle at the head of the Institute he founded.

However that may be, De La Salle did leave his mountain retreat, probably in June 1713, and headed for Mende, far to the west, where the community appeared to be in deep trouble. Neither the original biographers nor contemporary authors seem to agree on who was to blame for what happened, although there is a certain consistency in the accounts. The villain of the piece seems to have been a certain Brother Medard. After being transferred from Calais to Marseille in 1708 and from there to Grenoble, he decided to leave the Institute. Welcomed back by De La Salle in 1712 at Marseille, he again took the habit in the novitiate there and, perhaps, became identified with the malcontents. Sent from Marseille to the school at Mende, he soon resumed his errant ways. He gradually won over his companion, Brother Isidore, to an easy lifestyle and to extensive social contacts contrary to the letter and the spirit of the Common Rule. Meanwhile, a dispute arose between two other Brothers, Henri and Bernardin, as to which had the rightful claim to be the Director, a dispute that the sources leave unresolved to this day. The tendency has been to consider Brother Henri the interloper, but this may be due to the fact that later on Brother Isidore carried back to Paris his version of his difficulties with Henri as Director. To make matters worse, Brother Ponce, who as regional superior should have dealt with the situation, was on his way back to Rouen where he soon left the Institute.

When news reached Mende that De La Salle was on his way, Brothers Medard and Isidore hurried to the bishop and the mayor to get their support for maintaining the status quo. Thus the Founder was utterly frustrated when he arrived in trying to deal effectively with the problem. He did not want to alienate the new bishop, Pierre Baglion de La Salle (no relative), by insisting on the Institute policy of assigning Brothers where they could achieve the most good. The bishop and the mayor, on the other hand, were adamant in insisting that the Brothers not be transferred; in the six years since the school had opened too many Brothers had already been sent elsewhere or had left the Institute.

To add insult to injury, De La Salle was told point blank that he could not be accommodated in the Brothers' house and that the community did not have the resources to provide his meals. Forced to seek hospitality with the Capuchins for a time, the Founder was invited to stay at the house of Mlle. Lescure, Foundress of the Ladies of the Christian Union, a new congregation similar in many respects to that of the Brothers. De La Salle was happy to be able to assist her in composing a rule for these sisters. Otherwise, during the two months that he stayed in Mende, he remained again in solitude and prayer, isolated from his Brothers.

During this time, Brother Timothy came to Mende looking for his Superior. Turned away from the community of the Brothers as the

Founder had been, he found De La Salle at the Lescure house. He brought the news that the Marseille novitiate was now completely empty of novices and he asked for a new assignment for himself. Blain, probably working from notes supplied by Brother Timothy himself, quotes the Founder's touching reply: "Why do you come to me with all of this? Don't you know that I am not competent to give orders to others? Are you not aware that there are many Brothers who no longer want to have anything to do with me? They say they no longer want me as their superior. And they are right: I am really incapable of that any more."

Mlle. Lescure meanwhile was trying to induce De La Salle to settle permanently in Mende, promising to provide him with room and board for life and, after his death, to subsidize another Brother for the school. Perhaps encouraged by Brother Timothy's visit and his expressions of loyalty, De La Salle refused the tempting offer, still uncertain as to what he should do with so many problems unresolved. When it came time for him to leave Mende, the good lady provided him with a horse to make the long journey back to Avignon and Grenoble less painful.

After the departure of the Founder, the situation of the Mende community deteriorated even further. Brother Medard left the city without authorization to go to Avignon but he died en route in the community at Ales. Brother Isidore, as noted above, went to Paris where he reported his version of the events to Brother Barthelemy who evidently believed him. Brother Henri remained in Mende, for a time alone. Father Martineau, the pastor at Mende, skipping over Brother Barthelemy who was supposedly in charge of the Brothers in the capital, wrote instead to the priests of Saint Sulpice to get replacements for the Brothers who had left. Fortunately, it was just at this time in 1714 that De La Salle had decided to obey the command of the Paris Brothers and return to take over the active direction of the Institute. Two Brothers were sent to Mende to work with Brother Henri in the school. Eventually Brother Henri and his companion Brother Nicolas gave their lives working heroically with the victims of the plague that devastated Mende in 1721.

But that is to get ahead of the story. It is no exaggeration to say that in 1713 the Institute was facing a severe crisis. Brother Barthelemy, nominally in charge in Paris, was too timid to resist the escalating efforts of the parish priests of Saint Sulpice to control the Society. Brother Ponce had left the South in a shambles and Brother Timothy at Avignon was hard put to pick up the pieces. The Founder was thoroughly discouraged. In his too great willingness to blame himself whenever anything went wrong, he preferred to keep himself out of the picture and to find guidance in solitude and prayer.*

In this frame of mind, there was still one place in the South that De La Salle had yet to visit and that was the school at Grenoble. After that there might be time to resolve the serious problem of what his future role with the Brothers might be. He arrived in Grenoble toward the end of the summer of 1713. He needed time to think things through from the beginning, to restore his energy, so spent from all the disputes and persecution, so battered by the many reverses he had suffered. Grenoble proved to be a place where he could retire for a time in peace and tranquility. The Brothers teaching there in the school of Saint Laurent were happy to receive their spiritual father for the first time. With the dedication of true sons they did all they could to relieve the sufferings of his heart.

Once he was settled in Grenoble, De La Salle turned his attention to the revision of his published works. Maillefer tells us that he was particularly anxious to rework *The Duties of a Christian* since he had made this a basic text for all the schools. He was able to give attention to some of his spiritual writings as well. Once the revisions were complete he obtained official approval from the papal legate at Avignon to have them reprinted. During this time also he carefully revised the specifics of the daily schedule which the Brothers were to follow. This was to serve later as the basis for the definitive text of the Rule of the Brothers.

Aware that he was only a short distance away from the monastery of the Grande Chartreuse, De La Salle decided to interrupt his work to go to make a retreat there. This would have been during the school vacation period at the end of August or the beginning of September 1713. The Carthusians had a special meaning for De La Salle because Saint Bruno, their Founder, had been, like himself, a canon of the cathedral chapter of Reims. Taking another Brother with him as a companion, De La Salle expressly forbade him to reveal their identity. The two pilgrims were cordially received by the monks. But the piety of the one betrayed his identity more than any indiscretion on the part of

---

*NOTE: This concludes the section interpolated into the Burkhard account to fill in the details of the difficulties that De La Salle encountered in the South and that eventually led him to Parmenie. What follows incorporates into the body of the text some of the material that forms part of an appendix in Burkhard's *Parménie*. —BLS.

the other. The memory of this brief visit was still alive many years later when two other Brothers went to the Chartreuse for a similar retreat. We have the testimony of a certain Brother Patrice in a deposition written for the process of beatification:

> During the month of September 1781, two of us, the Brother Director of Grenoble and myself, went to spend a few days at the Grande Chartreuse. We were received with signs of distinction. These famed solitaries told us that the deep-rooted virtue of our venerable Founder was still admired in their solitary retreat and that the lapse of sixty-six years had not effaced the memory of it. The Father Prior and the Father Procurator, themselves worthy and respected men, told us that their priests had been so struck by the holiness and goodness of our Founder that they had begged him to remain with them. But the modesty of the humble priest betrayed his identity. Since he had wanted to remain at the monastery only on condition that he be totally unknown, De La Salle left the Chartreuse and returned to the community of the Brothers.

It is possible that De La Salle might also have visited Parmenie during this same vacation period but there is no evidence for it. Even supposing that he might have encountered Sister Louise, it is hardly possible that he would have made a special trip with the sole purpose of meeting her. On the contrary, during this period he was avoiding outside contacts as much as possible, even with his many friends in Grenoble.

Shortly after the opening of school in September 1713, De La Salle became troubled at the news that a schism might be brewing among the Brothers in the North. He sent Brother Jacques, the Director of the school in Grenoble, to investigate. He was a holy man, dependable, discreet, and much attached to his vocation. De La Salle commissioned him to verify the nature and seriousness of the situation and instructed him on how to apply the appropriate remedies. The departure of the Brother Director left a serious gap in the teaching staff of the school. This De La Salle proceeded to fill himself by taking over the Director's classes. Here was new evidence of his zeal for the children that he loved so well: De La Salle himself as one of their teachers.

The impression that De La Salle made on the townspeople of

Grenoble was profound according to the testimony of the aforementioned Brother Patrice in his deposition to the authorities at Rome:

> I was sent to the community of Grenoble in 1780 and here is what I learned in that city. Father De La Salle performed there all the ordinary functions of a schoolteacher and did so with inexpressible joy. He himself led his students to the parish church where he celebrated Mass for them. The students, and especially anyone who served his Mass, were all struck with the piety and devotion of this priest. Whenever he was spotted on his way to the church with his young scholars, people could be heard to say: "Let us go to Mass. See, there, the holy priest on his way to celebrate it." I myself heard these words as they were quoted to me by the old men of the city who had been pupils of De La Salle.

For the most part, however, De La Salle remained in seclusion during this period, the winter of 1713-1714. There is a plaque posted on the front of the building at 40 Rue Saint Laurent in Grenoble which to this day identifies his hideaway. Brother Yves Poutet has recently described it in these words: "There is the ancient granite stairway, the wooden balcony overlooking an inner courtyard, the small apartment in the recess of the isolated tower. All of this serves as a vivid reminder of the man who transformed the system of elementary education for all of France." This, then, is the place that De La Salle selected to pray in solitude and to revise his writings, "the least comfortable and most remote room in the house," to quote Canon Blain. And it was in the oratory of the community, a small room set aside for prayer where three people could scarcely be squeezed in, that he passed a good part of each day.

Soon the long hours of work and prayer in this miserable "hole in the wall" took their toll. In the month of February 1714, De La Salle began to experience new and acute attacks of rheumatism which increasingly caused him agonizing pain. For a time it was thought he might die. Once again he endured the extreme and very painful remedy that had been used once before in Paris. Developed by a Dutch doctor named Helvetius, this treatment consisted in stretching the patient over a sort of grill beneath which were medicinal herbs steaming over burning coals. Painful as the remedy was, it was effective and the Founder gradually recovered.

During the convalescence, according to the biographers, the whole city of Grenoble became concerned about his recovery. Prayers were offered everywhere as if for an important matter of public interest. His close friends were especially worried, in particular, Yse de Saleon and Claude Canel, the two canons of the church of Saint Andre who had been instrumental in bringing the Brothers to Grenoble. The general rejoicing once De La Salle was out of danger was clear evidence that the inhabitants of Grenoble had been completely won over by the dedication and humility of this holy priest.

As soon as he felt that he was regaining his strength, De La Salle began to think about making another spiritual retreat. It is possible, also, now that he had fulfilled his responsibility by visiting all of the houses of the Institute, that he wanted time to think through a decision that had been troubling him for a long time. He had to decide whether the time had come for him to seek out some solitary place where he might retire and remove himself permanently from the direction of his Institute.

It seemed to him that perhaps the moment had come. His friend, the Canon Yse de Saleon, encouraged him to spend several days in the solitude of Parmenie. De La Salle accepted the invitation eagerly. Even though it was still toward the end of the winter season, the stay at Parmenie proved to be beneficial to his health. This was a source of satisfaction to his host. On the other hand, De Saleon was worried that zeal for the apostolate might force De La Salle to leave his retreat much too soon, once he felt that his strength had returned. Accordingly De Saleon took advantage of some urgent business that needed his attention in Provence as an excuse to ask De La Salle to replace him as the director of the Parmenie retreats during his absence. This gave De La Salle a way of expressing gratitude to his host and, at the same time, satisfying his attraction for the solitary life. He thought, too, that this might be the answer from heaven that he had been waiting for over a long time. In truth, there was reason to wonder why it was that Providence had brought him all the way from Paris to the solitude of this mountain retreat.

From Parmenie he could see the peaks of the Chartreuse range, the naked white rocks of Chalves and the barren Chamechaude. Looking out on this spectacular view day after day, enjoying the calm such moments brought to him, De La Salle began to feel within himself a reawakening of sad and anxious thoughts. Should he not quit the world altogether and follow the example of Saint Bruno who, like himself, had resigned his lucrative canonry at Reims? Could he not give greater honor and glory to God by directing the spiritual retreats at Parmenie instead of struggling against the never-ending obstacles put in his way by his jealous and hateful enemies?

In this frame of mind, De La Salle might well have thought that he had done all that he could to accomplish his mission in founding the Institute. He had written a great deal and so could leave to the Brothers an adequate legacy to guide them in their religious and professional life. There were more than thirty establishments all over France. Furthermore, he had always thought that the Brothers should be governed by one of their own rather than by a priest like himself.

He was open, therefore, to the possibility that the moment might have come to leave to itself the work he had started. For him, the best indication that this might be the right approach was the series of bitter persecutions that seemed to have been directed against him personally. Now the Lord had brought him to Parmenie. No sooner had he tasted the charms of that solitude when he felt himself inevitably drawn to the prospect of spending the last days of his life there.

He shared with Sister Louise these perplexities that were troubling his soul. "That is not God's will for you," she said. "In no way should you abandon the family God has given you. It is your vocation to work actively. You must persevere in it even unto death, combining as you have up to now the life of Mary and Martha."

This reply is the more remarkable for its disinterestedness since at that very moment Sister Louise was looking for a new director for the Parmenie retreats. Father Roux had recently died and Canon Saleon was busy with too many other projects. She certainly saw in John Baptist de La Salle the ideal sort of priest who would have made a marvelous retreat director. But two unexpected events were to manifest rather clearly the ways of divine Providence.

During the time that De La Salle was in the Dauphiny country, things were not going at all well back in Paris. His adversaries took advantage of the Founder's absence to meddle in the government of his Institute, tampering with those things he considered essential, including the Rule and the Constitutions. Faced with such a serious situation, the Directors and principal Brothers of the Paris region decided upon a rather extreme course of action. They drew up a joint communication in which they addressed De La Salle and orderd him to return in virtue of the vow he had made to obey the body of the Society. Composed with unprecedented boldness, yet admirable in its simplicity, this document is one of the most touching tributes that the Institute ever paid to its

Founder and the most striking proof of its unalterable fidelity to him. The letter was delivered to De La Salle at his mountain retreat in the Dauphiny.

> Monsieur, our very dear Father: We the principal Brothers of the Christian Schools, having in view the greater glory of God as well as the good of the Church and of our Society, consider that it is of the greatest importance that you return to the care and general direction of God's holy work, which is also your own, because it has pleased the Lord to make use of you to establish it and guide it for so many years.
>
> We are all convinced that God himself has called you to this work and that he has given you the grace and talents necessary for the good government of this new Society so beneficial to the Church. We acknowledge in all justice that you have always guided it with considerable success and edification. That is why, Monsieur, we very humbly beseech you, and we command you in the name and on the part of the body of the Society to which you have vowed obedience, to take up at once the general government of our Society.

The letter was signed by all the Brothers present and De La Salle recognized the signatures of his sons. Clearly, there was no alternative. He was still their Founder, their superior and father; his vast family had need of him. When, at last, he showed the directive to Sister Louise, she replied in this judicious way:

> You know as well as anyone, Father, that it is not enough for you to speak of the virtue of obedience as one of the mainstays of your Institute. The best rule for you is to begin to practice what you have preached to others. It is evident that the Lord wants you to return to Paris and to give yourself to your Brothers. You will be free to do that as soon as Father Saleon returns to resume the direction of the house and has had a chance to thank you for all the fine things you have done here during his absence. My advice is that you hesitate no longer to accomplish what God clearly wants you to do in this matter.

De La Salle hesitated no longer and agreed to follow the wise counsel of Sister Louise. But then, just a short time before he was ready to leave, another event occurred that confirmed his decision all the more.

There came to Parmenie just at this time a young pilgrim dressed in the humble costume of the Dauphiny peasants. But underneath this ragged exterior was a man of honorable family and distinguished upbringing. His name was Claude Dulac, the son of Claude Lancelot Dulac de Montisambert. He had entered military service at the age of fifteen and was well liked by his fellows for his charm, his generosity and his courage. However he soon became taken up with the pursuit of pleasure. He developed a passion for gambling and lost considerable sums at it. Seriously wounded at the battle of Malplaquet in September 1711, he began to reflect on his past extravagances. His long convalescence gave him the time he needed to determine to mend his ways and break with his gambling friends. Within a short time he became known in his regiment as a model of exactitude, good order and honesty.

At the age of twenty-two, after he had been in military service as an officer for eight years, he arranged to resign his commission without notifying in advance either his family or his many friends. In the guise of a peasant he set out on a long pilgrimage that eventually brought him to Grenoble. There he lived a life devoted to works of charity, especially in the hospitals where he performed the most menial services for the sick.

It was no mere chance that he should meet Father Claude Canel who had worked harder than anyone to establish the hospital in Grenoble, he himself directing it for many years. It was there that Dulac also met Father De Saleon and soon made a retreat under his direction. De Saleon, who had just returned from his tour of Provence, invited Dulac to accompany him to Parmenie where the young man might consult with John Baptist de La Salle. De Saleon knew that Dulac had already tried in vain to enter the Chartreuse, and before that the Franciscans, and that he was still anxiously trying to discover his true vocation.

De La Salle held long conversations with the young ex-officer. After much thought, and after consulting with Canon De Saleon, the Founder decided to accept Dulac as a member of the Institute of the Brothers. Accordingly, he returned to the community in Grenoble, taking the young man with him. There the Founder invested him with the habit of the Society on June 6, 1714 and gave him the name Brother Irenee. As things turned out, this new disciple of De La Salle was to become one of the most influential and best known members of the

Institute as Director of Novices, Director of the motherhouse at St. Yon and Assistant to the Superior General.

Shortly after his encounter with this new recruit, De La Salle left the Dauphiny country to take in hand once again the direction of his Institute. The influence of Sister Louise had been decisive. If she had kept him at Parmenie, as her urgent need for a retreat director and De La Salle's personal love for solitude would seem to have suggested, the whole educational enterprise of De La Salle might well have collapsed. It was the return of De La Salle to Paris that saved the Institute of the Brothers of the Christian Schools from almost certain ruin.

Although De La Salle had only five years to live after his departure from Parmenie, there was time enough for him to consolidate his work, to determine its final form and definitive rule. Shortly before his death he had the consolation of seeing one of his most ardent desires realized in the election of one of his own disciples, Brother Barthelemy, as Superior General. De La Salle died on April 7, 1719. Today the Institute of the Brothers of the Christian Schools is one of the most important in the Church devoted exclusively to the apostolate of education. It is rather paradoxical to think that this development is due, in part at least, to a poor shepherdess who herself had no formal education at all.

If the work of De La Salle continued to prosper after the death of its Founder, that was not the case, unfortunately, with the work established at Parmenie by Sister Louise. Her providential encounter with De La Salle seems to have been the high point in the history of the place. Everything after that has been a story of progressive decline, right up until the very recent past.

CHAPTER IV

Unresolved Questions Concerning De La Salle
at Parmenie

This chapter, authored by Luke Salm, substitutes for the second appendix of the original French version of Burkhard's Parménie. *While raising the same questions to be found in that appendix, and drawing on the same source material, the attempt here is to examine in a wider context Burkhard's fundamental thesis on the significance of Parmenie for the spiritual journey of John Baptist de La Salle and the destiny of his Institute. The source materials are the same as those used in the previous chapters, with the notable addition of insights drawn from Chapter IV of the doctoral dissertation of Brother Miguel Campos, F.S.C., entitled "Effacement pour le bien de la Société des Frères des Ecoles Chrétiennes" and published in the* Cahiers lasalliens, *Volume 45, pages 288-306.*

In an appendix to *Parménie,* Brother Leo Burkhard addresses in a critical way two questions: 1) Why did the Founder remain for such a long time (more than two years) away from the Brothers in Paris at a time when the very existence of the Institute was threatened? 2) How much of this extended sojourn in the South was actually spent at Parmenie? The same questions could be put more sharply in this fashion: 1) Was De La Salle thinking seriously of leaving the Institute to spend his last days in retirement and solitude? 2) Once he had decided to obey the command of the Brothers to resume the direction of the Institute, why did it take so long (four months) for him to return to Paris?

As is clear from the previous chapters, it is Burkhard's thesis that De La Salle was indeed considering the possibility of leaving the Institute to its own fate in order to remain permanently in seclusion at Parmenie or elsewhere; that it was Sister Louise who helped him to decide otherwise and obey the command of the Brothers to return; that the Institute was in such a troubled state at the time that it probably

The Parmenie chapel in ruins in 1960 prior to the restoration. The area to the rear that now serves as a sanctuary was originally the sacristy and it is most probable that De La Salle had his room there during his stay at Parmenie. The underground crypt where Sister Louise was buried was discovered under the rubble in the foreground of the photograph.

would not have survived if the Founder had not so decided. In this vein, Burkhard concludes his discussion of De La Salle at Parmenie with these words: "It was on the hill of Parmenie, not far from Grenoble, that the fate of his young Institute was decided once and for all." It might be useful and interesting, therefore, to examine the sources more deeply to illuminate and possibly nuance this interpretation of the events described in the previous chapters.

The early biographers seem to support this thesis as they trace what may be called a pattern of withdrawal in the movements of De La Salle during the critical period from 1712 to 1714. A case in point would be the very decision to leave Paris while the judgment was still pending in the Clement affair. The failure of the pastors of Saint Sulpice and Saint Denis to come to the rescue of the Founder was but one more instance of an ongoing effort on the part of the ecclesiastics in Paris to bring the Society of the Brothers under clerical control. De La Salle himself began to wonder whether his continued presence among the Brothers would not do more harm than good. There was no need to await the final judgment in the Clement affair: without support or defense, betrayed by his own attorney, already deprived of the right to teach, he knew what the verdict would be. According to Blain, his greatest suffering at this moment was caused by the impression he had that the majority of the Brothers in Paris were beginning to side with those who wanted to impose another form of government on the Society. As Blain puts it, with a feeling of abandonment by his Brothers and conscious of the silence of Jesus before his accusers, but also blaming no one but himself and thinking only of the good of the Institute, De La Salle left Paris for the South of France at the beginning of Lent in 1712.

Arriving in the port city of Marseille, the Founder was well received at first. As we have seen in the previous chapter, he became actively engaged in the affairs of the Institute, opening a novitiate and planning for new schools in all parts of the city. After an initial period of unprecedented success and enthusiastic support, the opposition to his policies began to gather force. The issues were much the same: a preference for ecclesiastics in the schools and control by local pastors, with many of the Brothers siding with the townspeople who supported that view. Again, De La Salle decided to withdraw, this time to a hermitage some distance from the city where he endured what the biographers call "the dark night of the soul." Maillefer quotes the Founder as saying: "I was convinced that my absence would calm my enemies and inspire them to think positively about my spiritual children."

Blain describes this as a time when the Founder saw himself at the crossroads, full of doubts as to which way to turn. Both biographers mention the rumors that were circulating in Marseille to the effect that the Founder had already abandoned the Brothers. While this was not true, and the authors are careful to refute the story, they do admit that it had some basis in the possibilities that De la Salle had been considering for himself.

After leaving his retreat outside Marseille, probably in June of 1713, De La Salle went to Mende, the westernmost outpost of the Institute. Repulsed by the Brothers there, who were either unwilling or unable to lodge him in the house, he again went into seclusion, at first with the Capuchins and later in the house of Mlle. Lescure where he remained for more than two months.

It was either in the hermitage outside Marseille or in the home of Mlle. Lescure in Mende that the very significant interview with Brother Timothy, described in the last chapter, took place. To begin with, the biographers emphasize the difficulty Timothy had in finding out where the Founder was. Both Blain and Maillefer cite verbatim the words of the Founder who said among other things that he felt he was no longer capable of fulfilling the role of Superior. Blain places this incident at Mende. There is good reason to accept his account and the authenticity of the quotation since Blain was writing under the direction of the same Brother Timothy, by that time Superior General, the person to whom the poignant words of the Founder were addressed.

Maillefer's version of this incident is perhaps even stronger. He locates it at Saint Maximin outside Marseille rather than at Mende. In this version, the Founder says to Timothy (who, incidentally, is not named but described as the Superior of the Novitiate at Marseille) that "he was surprised" that the Brothers were still thinking about him; that "he had hoped by leaving Marseille and retiring into solitude that people would soon get used to forgetting about him altogether"; that he found his hideaway so much to his liking that "he was resolved to stay hidden there and to condemn himself to perpetual silence." According to Maillefer, it took all of Timothy's powers of persuasion to convince De La Salle that the Brothers still needed him and wanted him to continue at the head of the Society.

In any event, De La Salle did leave his hideaway outside Marseille and, after a time, eventually left Mende to make his way to the house of the Brothers at Grenoble. But even here, Maillefer again stresses De La

Salle's desire to remain aloof, albeit within the community of the Brothers. Thus he says:

> He withdrew to Grenoble where he found the Brothers very much at peace. He resolved to stay with them as long as he could. He chose the most remote and least accessible room in the house where he could devote himself to mental prayer. He remained there for several months, unknown and practically forgotten. He made no visits, received no visitors and left his room only to be present at the scheduled time for the usual exercises of the community.

Thus De La Salle remained, most probably from August of 1713 until February of 1714, present among the Brothers yet remaining aloof.

It was during his stay in Grenoble, probably in September of 1713, that De La Salle took advantage of the proximity of the cloistered monastery of the Grande Chartreuse to go there with another Brother to make a retreat. His stay was interrupted by the fact that his identity became known. The biographers seem to imply that he would have preferred to stay longer if his plans to remain hidden and unknown had not been thwarted by the discovery of his identity. The opportunity for a more prolonged retreat came early in the following year, 1714, when, after his recovery from an acute attack of rheumatism, he came to Parmenie where he remained to serve as chaplain replacing his friend, Father Yse de Saleon. It is perhaps not an exaggeration to say with Burkhard that it was at Parmenie that his penchant for withdrawal into solitude came closest to becoming permanent.

Despite this pattern of withdrawal, however, there is another aspect to the Founder's activity during his stay in the South. While he may very well have been considering the possibility of permanent retirement from the Institute, De La Salle did continue to involve himself in its affairs. This was especially the case in Grenoble where he spent part of his time preparing new editions of his writings for the Brothers; he sent a Brother to Paris to find out what might be the state of affairs among the Brothers in the capital; he took over the classes of that Brother during his absence; he regularly led the pupils to the parish church where he celebrated Mass for them; he deputized some trusted Brothers to visit the other houses in Provence. There are also administrative letters from this period addressed to Brother Gabriel Drolin in Rome and to Brother Joseph in Reims.

Furthermore, the biographers are careful to emphasize the Founder's motivation in any consideration he might have been giving to withdrawing into seclusion. Such a possibility was not in any way motivated by weariness or discouragement, self pity, surrender to the opposition, or even his own attraction for prayer and solitude. Such motives would have been inconsistent with what we know of his character. A clue to the approach he would have brought to his dilemma can be found in a series of resolutions he drew up for himself at an earlier time. Among these resolutions the following is significant:

> I shall always consider the work of my salvation and the work of establishing and directing the Institute as the work of God. That is why I leave the care for this work entirely in his hands; I will do nothing for my part except by God's orders. I shall always consult extensively about what I should do, whether it concerns my own salvation or the Institute. I shall often address God in the words of Habacuc: *Domine, opus tuum;* Lord, the work is yours.

It is not surprising, therefore, that De La Salle might have come to blame himself for the troubles within the Institute and the opposition from without. It would be most characteristic of him to begin to wonder what the events of his life were telling him about God's will and if he himself might be an obstacle to the designs of Providence.

An element that would have made the agony of decision even more intense for the Founder was his commitment to the Society by vow. In 1691 De La Salle and two other Brothers had vowed to stay together in order to found the Institute even if they had to live on bread alone, the "heroic vow" as it has been called. The conditions of the vow would seem to have been fulfilled by the time the principal Brothers gathered at Vaugirard in 1694. On that occasion, however, De La Salle again vowed to unite himself and "to remain in Society with the Brothers to keep together and by association gratuitous schools," which vows he promised to keep inviolably all his lifetime.

In his study of the Founder's spiritual odyssey, Brother Miguel Campos provides a penetrating insight into the characteristic way in which De La Salle was able to relate his religious vision to his personal experience. Referring to the reversals at Marseille, Campos remarks:

> The impact of these events would have been extremely dramatic since they touched De La Salle at the heart of his personal identity, namely, the awareness that he had been called to a special mission. He was conscious of this vocation

as early as 1682. It had uprooted him from the world he knew to incarnate him in the unfamiliar world of the schoolteachers and the poor. The shock of these new reversals was soul-shattering: in effect these developments called into question the irrevocable decision he expressed by the vows of 1691 and 1694. The doubts that De La Salle experienced touched him intimately but not in any individualistic sense of the word. De La Salle had a keen awareness of what association meant since he experienced it in a profound way by sharing the mission of the Brothers during long years of difficulty and struggle. Accordingly, his doubts took the form of a prophetic critique or, perhaps better, a prophetic self-examination into his personal charism and mission.

According to Campos, it was with this mind that De La Salle asked himself whether his continued presence as the Superior of the Society and his inflexible attitudes as to how it should function were not indeed the source of the opposition from within and from without. If God were indeed asking him to abandon the Brothers for some form of parish work, it would not be for the downfall of the Society, but rather to remove himself as the obstacle to its consolidation. The Founder was not merely passive in the face of what was happening, but he was searching actively and relentlessly to discover what it was that the Lord required of him. It was in this sense that he was willing to entertain the possibility that perhaps God no longer wished him to remain among the Brothers.

There is evidence enough in the situations that developed at Paris, Marseille and Mende to show that in thinking along these lines De La Salle was not the victim of illusion or of self-enclosed subjectivism. Campos describes the situation as the Founder saw it in very plain terms:

> De La Salle found himself abandoned by his Brothers. The vow of association that had united them in a common adventure for the sake of a common mission now seemed to be called into question by the fact that the Brothers had abandoned him. To be abandoned by the Brothers was to be abandoned by God. The religious experience of De La Salle, his "dark night of the soul," to use the term traditional in spirituality, was not the product of some unhistorical abstraction. It arose from the very warp and woof of the events

of his life. Any questions he may have entertained about his role in the Society cannot be dissociated from the lofty vision that he had of his mission as God's work, of his awareness of his own sinfulness, and also of the fact that he had indeed been abandoned by the very men who had made with him the vow of association.

In some ways these reflections turn the question around: Was De La Salle abandoning the Brothers or were they abandoning him?

The facts make clear that De La Salle did not come to any hasty decision, agonizing as the doubts may have been and however earnest the soul-searching. The opportunities to share in the work of the Brothers and to give guidance where needed pulled him in one direction; the opportunities for prolonged periods of prayer and solitude pulled him in another. It is significant that it was precisely the terms of the vow of 1694 to obey "the Body of the Society" that settled his doubts and clarified for him what it was the Lord was asking him to do. The letter from the Brothers in Paris ordering him to return assured him that the Brothers had not in fact abandoned him. That his response may have been determined at Parmenie and supported by the advice of Sister Louise lends credibility to Brother Leo Burkhard's interpretation of the encounters that took place on that holy hill.

Subsequent events seemed to show that De La Salle had read the signs of the divine will aright. His withdrawl for rather long periods from the center of the controversies in Paris, Marseille, Mende and Grenoble had the desired effect. The attempt on the part of the parish priests in Paris to intervene in the government of the Society and to change it radically came to nothing. In fact, this served to solidify the determination of the Brothers to retain the independent and centralized structure that the Founder had established for them. Within three years the lost momentum had been regained to the point where De La Salle could confidently relinquish the office of Superior to Brother Barthelemy. In Marseille, although the Jansenist controversy became increasingly intense, the Brothers were left undisturbed and they continued to prosper since the Founder had been wise enough to warn them to keep aloof from ecclesiastical and theological disputes that did not directly concern them. The difficulties at Mende and the disruption that followed on the departure of Brother Ponce and other malcontents were likewise resolved in due course, with the firm and competent hand of Brother Timothy bringing new vigor and organization to the foundations in the South. In all of this, Providence seemed to confirm that De La Salle's decisions—both the decision to withdraw for a time and the decision to return—were the right ones.

A second question that understandably enough engages Brother Leo Burkhard in his appendix to *Parménie* is the problem of how much time De La Salle actually spent at the retreat center there. A closer look at the sources subdivides this question into two others that are somewhat more precise: 1) Was De La Salle at Parmenie when the command came from the Brothers in Paris to resume the direction of the Institute? 2) Once De La Salle received the command and agreed to obey (in April, 1714) why did it take him until August 10 to arrive in Paris?

The early biographers, careless and inconsistent as they are in matters of chronology, seem unconcerned about these problems. Both Blain and Maillefer speak of an initial sojourn at Parmenie for a retreat that lasted fifteen days during which, they say, De La Salle had extensive interviews with Sister Louise. Both refer to subsequent and multiple exchanges but are characteristically vague as to their circumstances and duration. Maillefer says that these consultations involved an exchange of letters, even though in the very next sentence he notes that Sister Louise did not know how to read. Although both biographers cite the advice of Sister Louise that the Founder should return to the work to which God had destined him, neither of them relate this advice to the command from the Brothers in Paris. In fact they seem to presume that the letter of April 1 reached De La Salle at Grenoble and that his decision to obey went contrary to the advice that he received there from Yse de Saleon and his other friends. De La Salle is then described as saying a sad and prayerful farewell to his friends in Grenoble, setting out shortly thereafter for Paris with stopovers at Lyon to venerate the relic of Francis de Sales and at Dijon to visit the Brothers. Blain simply dates the Founder's arrival in Paris on the feast of St. Lawrence, August 10, 1714.

Evidence from other sources, however, complicate this rather straightforward scenario. First of all, the biographers of Sister Louise are at one in referring to a prolonged stay at Parmenie in the spring of 1714 during which De La Salle served as a replacement for Yse de Saleon who had been called away on other business to visit the cites of Provence. Burkhard finds a reason for the willingness of De La Salle to undertake this responsibility and to withdraw to the seclusion of Parmenie in the fact that the Bull *Unigenitus* condemning Jansenism had just been published in Grenoble:

Once again, he [De La Salle] used his courage and intelligence to defend the official doctrine of the Church and so provoked a new wave of opposition from the Jansenists. There arose against him in the Dauphiny a new series of attacks that were every bit as virulent as those that had earlier led him to flee from Provence. It is precisely at this moment that De La Salle again left Grenoble for Parmenie. It is altogether probable that he once again employed his favorite tactic of going into retreat in order to spare his disciples the trials and persecutions that threatened them and their work because of their relation to him.

This judgment seems to conform to what had already happened in similar circumstances in Paris and Marseille.

In the second place, the biographers of Sister Louise locate De La Salle at Parmenie when the critical letter of April 1, 1714 arrived from the Brothers in Paris. Thus Dom Bellanger, basing himself on Gras du Villard, the spiritual director at Parmenie in 1750 and a close friend of Yse de Saleon, says: "He [De La Salle] left the Brothers' community secretly . . . and settled down at Parmenie. While he was there he functioned as spiritual director and confessor, replacing Father Yse de Saleon whose business affairs required his presence elsewhere. But soon the Brothers of Paris, Versailles and Saint Denis, having learned where De La Salle was hiding, wrote him a letter calling for his return." Although both Blain and Maillefer agree in supposing that De La Salle showed the letter to Sister Louise, her response, as quoted by Bellanger, suggests a reason both for the presence of the Founder at Parmenie and why his return had to be delayed. In this account she is supposed to have said: "It is evident that it is the Lord's will that you should return to Paris . . . as soon as Father De Saleon returns to resume his functions as director of this retreat center."

There is another indisputable piece of evidence that was either unknown to the early biographers of De La Salle or passed over by them. This places De La Salle at Parmenie in late May or early June of 1714 on the occasion of the encounter there with Claude Dulac de Montisambert. The exact date when this young man received the religious habit and the name Brother Irenee is marked in the register of the Grenoble community: "Entered the Society on June 6, 1714."

Finally, there is a letter from Brother Barthelemy discovered during the nineteenth century by Brother Lucard in the archives of

Lozere. Addressed to the authorities at Mende and dated July 17, 1714, the acting Superior in Paris writes in part: "I have learned that Father De La Salle left Grenoble some weeks ago to visit the communities in Provence." This tantalizing bit of evidence says nothing of what communities were visited. Was De La Salle finally able to return to Marseille? Did he go only as far as Avignon, perhaps to consult with Brother Timothy or to strengthen the contacts with Rome? Were there new developments in Les Vans or Ales that seemed more urgent than the situation in Paris? Or was Brother Barthelemy confusing the "communities in Provence" with the stopovers enroute northward to Paris that were mentioned by Blain and Maillefer? At any rate, the expression "some weeks ago" in a letter dated July 17 would seem to verify the presence of De La Salle in the area of Grenoble (and Parmenie) at least as late as early June. All of this evidence, then, would seem to suggest that De La Salle was at Parmenie, with occasional visits to Grenoble, for the greater part of four months from February to June of 1714.

In conclusion it might be said that the questions raised in Burkhard's appendix to *Parménie* and developed at greater length in this present chapter remain to some extent unresolved. On the other hand there seems to be some evidence to support the claim that the "encounters at Parmenie" were extensive in duration and significant for the spiritual journey of John Baptist de La Salle and for the future of his Institute.

Before turning to consider in greater detail the encounter at Parmenie between the Founder of the Brothers and his protege who came to be known as Brother Irenee, it would not be inappropriate to conclude this discussion, as Burkhard does, by quoting from an address delivered at Grenoble in 1951 by a Father Girard on the occasion of the tercentenary of the Founder's birth:

> It was here, in our midst, in our Dauphiny, that the Saint found the one, or almost the only one, of his foundations that was for him a source of nothing but joy. It was here among us that he worked on his educational and spiritual writings. It was here that he worked at the humble task of teaching in an elementary school. It was here, in the midst of a terrible crisis in the Church, that he gave directives that would guarantee forever the doctrinal orthodoxy of his disciples. It was here that he recieved the indisputable evidence of the loyalty of his sons. It was here that he encountered the saintly soul of

Sister Louise who made it possible for him to hear the voice of God whose accents he had been searching everywhere to catch.

To this Burkhard himself adds that "it was there, not far from Grenoble on the hill of Parmenie, that De La Salle experienced those encounters out of which the future of his Institute was assured once and for all."

CHAPTER V

Claude Dulac (Brother Irenee) Comes to Parmenie

This chapter is an original adaptation by Luke Salm of the anonymous Vie du Frère Irénée *published in 1930 by the* Procure Générale *of the Brothers in Paris. In the archives of the motherhouse of the Brothers in Rome the authors are identified as Brothers Vincent Goudy and Charles Simmoneau, F.S.C. They died within a month of each other in 1946-47. Unfortunately the French original follows an outdated style of hagiography, with many pious reflections, naive speculation, and exhortations to the reader—all impossible of direct translation into a contemporary idiom. Hence this adaptation, organized to highlight the encounter at Parmenie that is the theme of the present volume.*

The first Vie du Frère Irénée *appeared in Avignon in 1774, twenty-seven years after his death. It was written by a Father De La Tour on the basis of letters and testimonials from the Brothers who had known Brother Irenee, many of them his former novices. A second edition was published in 1854 and a third at Paris in 1892. In 1898, Ernest Riviere published his* Vie de Claude François du Lac de Montisambert *which brought to light many precious details concerning the family of Lancelot Dulac. In 1927, the* Echo de la Loire, *an important daily newspaper of Nantes, ran a series of articles on Brother Irenee with the title* Qui l'Aura? *(Who Will Have Him?). Later published by the Brothers in booklet form under the same title, this material is more in the style of an historical novel with incidents embellished by imaginative detail and reconstructed dialogue.*

For all of its pieties, the biography from the Paris Procure that forms the basis for this chapter is relatively sober in presenting the essential facts. In addition to the earlier works of La Tour and Riviere, it professes to include supplementary details provided by Bishop D'Allaines of Orleans, as well as documents and correspondence that were still extant and available to the authors.

Claude Francois Dulac was born in 1691 in the family castle of Montisambert near Orleans in central France. It was in this very same year that John Baptist de La Salle and two of his Brothers, when it seemed as if their young Society could hardly survive, vowed to stay together to establish the Institute even if they were reduced to begging

Brother Irenee (Claude Francois Dulac de Montisambert) from a painting preserved at Parmenie but destroyed in the fire set by vandals in 1965.

and had to live on bread alone. The circumstances of the noble and wealthy Dulac family were quite otherwise. The father, Claude IV Lancelot Dulac held the title of Lord of Montisambert; the mother, Ergnoust de Beauviller was also from a noble family well connected at the royal court. When the newborn Claude was baptized in the parish church at Tigy-sur-Loire, his godfather was a noble Norman on his mother's side; his godmother was a devout maiden aunt on his father's side, much given to the service of the poor, including sponsorship of a charitable school in Orleans.

Claude's parents were such contrasting personalities that twentieth-century psychologists might be inclined to see in them the origins of the conflicts that the young Claude had later on to resolve. The father was a veteran of the wars, a man of austere and inflexible will. Convinced that a military career was all but a divinely appointed duty for the nobility, he had his sons trained to the knightly virtues of bravery, generosity, virility and, above all, exact obedience. In order to insure that no son of his would ever be attracted to a career in law or in the Church, the old man expressly forbade any of them to ever study Latin. In this respect, he was most successful with the oldest son, Alphonse, who lived up fully to the father's expectations and eventually became a captain in the Royal Champagne regiment.

By the way of contrast, and perhaps conflict, there were feminine influences that were brought to bear, especially on Claude and his younger brother Nicolas. The mother was gentle, affable, and deeply religious, always dignified but never ostentatious or aggressive. She loved her children and raised them in an atmosphere of piety and devotion, reminding them often of their obligation to have compassion for the poor. Sensing in the young Claude the drives of an ardent and passionate nature, she tried to develop in him a strong devotion to the Blessed Virgin so that he would instinctively turn to the Mother of God in times of temptation. In addition to a devoted mother, Claude had the example of the saintly aunt who had been his godmother, and his equally devout and self-sacrificing sister, Francoise Sylvie, both of whom died while he was still very young.

Claude was barely into his teens when his father decided it was time for him to begin his military career. Convinced that it did not require much formal schooling to learn how to mount a horse or brandish a sword, the father was content to leave Claude's education incomplete and, in fact, terribly inadequate for a person of his social status and wealth.

While these arrangements were being made for Claude's entrance into the army, his godmother lay dying. She said farewell in these words: "You are my spiritual son and I bless you. I offer my life for you that you may become a saint and a great one."

When the day of departure for the army arrived, the father gave terse and precise orders without any show of emotion. The mother, close to tears, said a tender farewell, giving traditional pieces of advice: never neglect to pray morning and evening; be courteous to all, help the poor, and observe moderation in eating and drinking; be faithful to your pledged word and never tell a lie. Thus in 1705, during the war of the Spanish Succession, Claude Dulac, aged fourteen, entered military service in the regiment of Saint Menehould.

It is not surprising that the young teenager, inexperienced and naive as he was, should little by little be seduced into a life of easy but elegant vice. Before long, he fell into the hands of professional swindlers; he gambled a great deal and lost considerable sums of money. Despite a generous allowance from his family, he was frequently in debt. At first the father was patient, simply warning the lad to be more careful. But soon the old man realized that he was only pouring his money into a bottomless well. He sent an order to his son to resign his commission and to return to Montisambert.

The young soldier obeyed. Instead of the harsh reproaches he expected from the family, he found only a discrete silence, touched perhaps by a note of sadness, and very little direct reference to his foolishness. Even the father seemed to understand that unbending rigor would only embitter this prodigal son, so proud in his youth and so thirsting for independence. The mother had her own subtle way of expressing confidence that her dear son would come to understand that a Montisambert ought to be ready to make any sacrifice to preserve honor and virtue. His young sister, too, knew how to lavish signs of affection on her wayward brother in the hope that her piety and devotion would prove attractive to him. Claude thus made his peace with God and with his conscience; gradually he fell into the family routine he had known as a child.

Before very long, however, it became clear that Claude was becoming bored with country life. The days seemed interminable. There was little to do except to ride off into the woods with his horse and his dogs. Sometimes he would push as far as the heights above the Loire where he could see the vast stretch of the river below with its prospect of adventure beyond. Then he would return home to the monotonous routine, more desolate and disheartened than ever.

It was not long until the father began to realize how urgent it was to rescue such a fine young nobleman from boredom and idleness. Accordingly, he bought for his son a commission as a lieutenant in the Royal Champagne regiment, the very same where his older brother was already a captain. There it was hoped that the brother and the many friends of the family among the officers would be able to keep an eye on the youngster. And so, at the age of eighteen, Claude Dulac reentered the military service and did so with evident joy. The officers celebrated his arrival with a feast, happy to welcome this handsome, distinguished and debonair young officer into their company.

Unfortunately, it wasn't long before Claude began to slip again into the pattern of pleasure and vice that he and his young companions found both available and attractive. Even more serious, the habit of compulsive gambling began once again to take hold of him. He was spending longer and longer hours at the gaming tables, losing consistently, pawning his possessions and going deeper and deeper into debt. Alerted to what was going on, the father this time cut off the allowance of the young prodigal at once and Claude soon found himself at the end of his resources. The anger, humiliation, fatigue, and lack of sleep soon took their toll. He fell seriously ill and word reached Tigy that he was close to death. The mother's pleas for mercy and pardon finally persuaded the father to relent. He wrote to the colonel of the regiment, asking him to take every means to restore the young lieutenant to health, agreeing to pay all expenses including the gambling debts. This had a telling effect on Claude who soon began to recover both in body and in soul. At the age of eighteen, he had learned his lesson once and for all.

Not long after his recovery, the Royal Champagne regiment was called up to join in the war of the Spanish Succession. In the famous battle of Malplaquet, on September 11, 1709, Claude suffered a severe bullet wound. Fortunately the bullet did not penetrate any vital organ, but the convalescence was long and painful. The experience on the battlefield where he witnessed the sudden death of many of his young friends, as well as his appreciation for the care and solicitude of his family, served to strengthen the resolve of the young lieutenant to mend his ways. He soon became a model officer, generous in the service of his regiment and those under his charge, courteous to all and solicitous for their needs. He returned to the regular practice of his religious duties. In particular, he showed a special preference for visiting shrines dedicated to the Blessed Virgin.

On one of these occasions, he secluded himself in a remote corner of a monastery church to pray in solitude. He became so absorbed in his prayer that he did not notice when the outer doors of the church were being locked. All at once he realized that the monks were gathering in their choir stalls to hear and criticize the practice sermon of a young novice. Claude waited quietly until the session was over and the monks departed, but the locked doors made it impossible to slip away unobserved. Surprised to find a young officer still in the church, the Superior invited him to stay for the evening meal. "Monsieur," he said, "please do us the honor of sharing our supper with us since you have already shared our sermon. You owe it to the young preacher."

After the grace before meals and a reading from Scripture, the Abbot gave a *Benedicamus* (permission to talk) in honor of "a soldier of the king, a defender of his country and a devout hearer of the preached word of God." Recreation followed in the garden where the brilliant uniform of the officer stood out like a blazing flame among the somber habits of the monks. As Claude was about to take his leave, the Abbot promised that the monks would pray for his success and for advancement in his military career. Claude is said to have replied, "Pray rather for my conversion. It is you, Fathers, who are the happy ones. It is more glorious to be in the service of God than to be in the service of the king." It was probably from this time on that Dulac began to entertain seriously the possibility of a monastic vocation.

In the year 1711, his young sister Francoise Sylvie died. Her heroic suffering and premature death had a profound effect on Claude. In July of the same year he himself had another close brush with death. During the battle of Denain, the Royal Champagne took part in the six-day siege of the town of Marchiennes. Leading his men into battle, Claude was reckless in exposing himself to danger. A superior officer had to pull him back from one particularly dangerous spot; seconds later a bullet felled the unfortunate soldier who had been put in his place. Disappointed, perhaps, that God did not seem to want the sacrifice of his life as an atonement for his sins, Claude began to think of other ways to lose his life that he might save it.

The first step would be to resign his commission and then seek admission to a monastery. But this raised a host of practical problems. For one thing, he was due to be promoted in rank almost any day. For another, he had no specific idea about what form of monastic life he should embrace or how to go about it. Above all, he knew instinctively that his father would oppose absolutely and block effectively any such move on his part. For that reason, he arranged to resign from the army without saying anything to his comrades or his family, not even to his brother who was in the same regiment. Thus, after eight years of military service, he resigned his commission, sold his horse, his gear, and his military uniform. His sword he broke into pieces. Then, dressed in civilian clothes, which he later exchanged for a beggar's rags, he set off on foot in his long search to find what the Lord's will might be in his regard.

He headed in the general direction of Rome, hoping that he might find there some enlightenment as to what the Lord wanted him to do. He stopped en route at shrines of the Blessed Virgin whenever he could, including the famous chapel at Fourvieres, high above the city of Lyon. He stayed for two weeks in the old town that had been evangelized in the second century by Saint Irenaeus (*Irénée* in French); the old town had also been host to two general councils of the Church in the thirteenth century. From Lyon, Claude went to nearby Grenoble where he spent six months working in the hospital and caring for the sick, helping with the most humble and most repugnant services.

It happened that while he was in Grenoble Dulac attended a triduum honoring a newly canonized Capuchin monk. He was so moved by the sermons preached on that occasion that he presented himself at the Capuchin monastery on the following day and asked to be admitted to the ranks of the lay brothers. The Father Guardian listened to his story, cautioned patience, and waited a full three months before agreeing to admit the young pilgrim to the novitiate.

Shortly thereafter the Guardian insisted that Claude write home to obtain his baptismal certificate and his father's consent that he enter the monastery. Claude had no choice but to obey, knowing full well that his father would never agree. To keep his hiding place secret, he had the letter sent from Switzerland and directed that the reply be sent to Italy to the Capuchin house in Modena. Respectful and deferential as the letter was, it nonetheless provoked a violent reaction in the old man. Using his considerable influence with the papal nuncio, the elder Dulac managed to obtain a papal order to conduct a search for his son in all of the Capuchin novitiates in France, Italy and Switzerland. When news of this reached the Father Guardian in Grenoble, he summoned the young novice to explain to him that it was necessary for the good of the monastery that he leave at once.

Where, then, to go? The Grande Chartreuse was not far from Grenoble and Claude thought he might possibly find the peace that he so desperately sought there among the sons of Saint Bruno. The Father Prior received him graciously enough and kept him for several days. But once he learned that the young man could produce neither his baptismal certificate nor his father's consent, he declared that it would be impossible to keep him any longer. Furthermore, he remarked that Claude had no knowledge of Latin. That was an additional obstacle. He was told, therefore, to finish his studies, to learn Latin, to obtain his father's consent, and then all obstacles to admission would disappear. So for a second time, Claude found himself outside the cloister door. He began to study Latin on his own but, finding that too difficult, he returned to his original plan and resumed his pilgrimage to Rome.

He went on his journey as a true pilgrim, unencumbered and without resources, begging for food and enduring the mockery of passersby. The road over the Alps was long and tiresome. He often felt lonely and isolated, tempted at times to give up the whole idea and return to his life of pleasure. But he persevered in his resolve. As he neared the end of his journey and saw in the distance the dome of Saint Peter's he prostrated himself on the ground and recited the Creed. After several days spent in visiting the principal churches and the traditional centers of pilgrimage in Rome, he set out once again on his return journey to France. Enroute he took time out for an extended period of prayer and meditation at the shrine of Our Lady of Loretto, asking Mary's help for guidance and courage to complete his quest.

He had barely returned to Grenoble when he fell seriously ill, worn out from the fatigue and privations of his long journey. Once he had sufficiently recovered his strength, Claude determined to try once again to enter a monastery, this time the Trappist Abbey of Sept-Fonds near Autun where he presented himself for admission. Sept-Fonds, hallowed by the memory of Saint Bernard centuries before, was still renowned for the austerity of its monks. After Claude was there for only three days, the Abbot summoned him to tell him point blank that he did not belong in the monastery. "God," he said, "is calling you to some new order. I don't know exactly which one but I have a feeling that you may be near the end of your search. Continue to pray, therefore, and be confident that since you are sincerely seeking to find God's will, you will surely find it." With that, the Abbot sent him away, imparting his own benediction and that of the Blessed Virgin Mary. Once again, disappointed but not discouraged, Claude Dulac heard the door of the monastery close behind him. He returned to Grenoble to await there some clue as to what God might have in store for him.

This time it occurred to him to seek out the advice of a local priest. There was in Grenoble at this time a holy and apostolic priest with a reputation for his unusual gifts of discernment and spiritual direction. This was none other than the Vicar General of the diocese of Grenoble, Father Jean Yse de Saleon, who was charged as well with the direction of the retreat center established by Sister Louise at Parmenie. He suggested that Claude go to Parmenie to spend a few weeks in retreat, devoting his time to prayer and also giving a hand with the service of the retreat center. De Saleon promised to come soon to Parmenie himself to see how things were progressing.

Meanwhile, John Baptist de La Salle had himself come to Parmenie where for some months he had been acting as a replacement for the Vicar General while he was away. And so it happened that Yse de Saleon had occasion to recommend the noble Montisambert to De La Salle. The Grenoble priest was able likewise to explain to his young protege the character of the Founder of the Brothers and the importance of the work of the schools. He even suggested that this might indeed be the new religious congregation where God was calling him to work out his salvation in peace and where he might accomplish much good for others. The Brothers were not altogether unknown to Dulac. He had seen them often enough in their black robes, white rabat, and mantle with hanging sleeves, most recently in Grenoble as they led their charges through the city streets. But he was not particularly attracted to them. His own lack of formal schooling, together with the privileged circumstances in which he had been brought up, were hardly likely to draw him to the lifestyle of an ordinary schoolmaster.

De La Salle, for his part, knew young people well. He was much impressed with this young gentleman whose religious spirit and dedication to the poor were admired by everyone in Grenoble. But once the Founder learned the story of the misspent youth of this young convert, the two years wandering as a pilgrim, the failure to gain admittance to several monasteries, the wise priest was hesitant at first to encourage him to join the new Society. De La Salle was afraid that he might have on his hands an inconstant spirit, a restless dreamer who loved change and variety, one who would never be able to adjust to the deadly routine that made up the ordinary life of the Brothers. There was the further question of whether a young nobleman would be content for very long to enclose himself in a community of men committed to a function that was held in such low esteem by society at large.

Meeting De la Salle at Parmenie, Father Yse de Saleon reassured his friend. He said that he knew the young man well and knew from experience that he was capable of great sacrifice. Furthermore, Claude wanted to live unknown, far from the world, his family, and his former companions. The Society of the Brothers would be ideal since it would be the last place anyone would think of looking for him. Indeed, De Saleon concluded, the day would come when De La Salle would thank him for recommending such an excellent subject. De la Salle accordingly took advantage of the quiet and isolation of Parmenie to hold prolonged interviews with the eager aspirant. In time the Founder was won over by the honesty and hope of the young man, as well as his enthusiasm for a life of perfection.

Before he gave his final approval, however, De La Salle decided to test the candidate's ability to obey. One day he told Claude to go to his room and to spend his time in prayer and reflection in the presence of God. He was to remain there in this attitude until De La Salle himself should come to question him further. Immediately and without a word, as if he had been given a command by a superior officer in the army, Dulac went to his small cell and began to pray with all his heart. Toward evening, the two priests met in the garden and De Saleon asked how the morning's interview had turned out. "I sent him to reflect before God on the consequences of his decision," said De La Salle. "Come along with me and let us see how he is doing." They found the young man still on his knees before the crucifix. When he saw De La Salle, Claude threw himself at the Founder's feet. He declared that he was now more convinced than ever that God wanted him to join the Society of the Brothers to do penance for his sins and to help save other young souls from falling into the same pitfalls. De La Salle brought him to his feet, embraced him and, with Yse de Saleon nodding approval, agreed to accept Claude Dulac into the congregation. From that moment on, there began to be forged a lasting bond between the two of them, the aging priest seeing in this young recruit, just twenty-three years old, a reflection of himself: the same willingness to sacrifice considerable temporal advantages to seek the will of God and to embrace the unlikely mission God had called them to accomplish.

Not long after these events, De La Salle brought his newest disciple down from the hill of Parmenie to the community of the Brothers at Grenoble and personally invested him with the religious habit. The young man was given the name Brother Irenee to replace the noble Montisambert name, which he had long since ceased to use, and his baptismal name of Claude Francois as well. His first biographer tells us that Claude's chestnut hair was at that time abundant and curly; not the least sacrifice the young novice had to make was to have it cut short in the style of the Brothers. These formalities served to bring to a conclusion and to guarantee permanence to the encounter at Parmenie between De La Salle and Dulac, an encounter that was to have great significance for the subsequent history of the Institute.

The novitiate formation of Brother Irenee was at first entrusted to the Brother Director at Grenoble. By this time, however, De La Salle had received the command from the principal Brothers in Paris to return to the capital and resume the direction of the Institute. Before leaving Grenoble he decided to send his newest novice to Avignon to complete his formation under the more experienced Brother Timothy. At Avignon, Brother Irenee was admired for his humility, his devoted-ness and his spirit of penance; he was an admirable new subject in every respect except one: he seemed totally unable to control the restless students in the classroom.

De La Salle was disturbed and disappointed when this news reached him. He then arranged to transfer Brother Irenee to Laon where he would be under the tutelage of Brother Andre, the most capable of the school directors at that time. But even this move failed to produce any improvement in the young Brother's ability to conduct a class. His manner was just too gentle and refined, while his aristocratic bearing and upbringing made it impossible for him to maintain with his young charges the firmness that classroom discipline requires.

We know from the extant replies in the collection of De La Salle's letters that Brother Irenee himself began to have serious doubts about the authenticity of his vocation. He seems even to have been tempted to consider the possibility of returning to the pleasures and the excitement of the life that he had long since left behind. The reassurance in the letters from his fatherly superior proved sufficient to calm his fears and to convince him that God indeed was calling him to accomplish much good in the Institute.

The practical problem of his failure in the classroom was resolved when De La Salle transferred Brother Irenee to the novitiate at Saint Yon to be Sub-Director under Brother Barthelemy. When that worthy Brother succeeded De La Salle as Superior General in 1717, Brother Irenee was appointed Director of Novices and Director General of the motherhouse at Saint Yon. In this capacity, it fell to the lot of Brother Irenee to attend De La Salle in his final illness and to close his eyes in death when the end finally came on April 7, 1719.

The momentum of the encounter at Parmenie did not end with the death of De La Salle. This is not the context to recount all the details of the subsequent history of Brother Irenee and his impact on the young Institute. In general it may be said that the Brothers regarded him as the living prolongation of the Founder, as the authentic source to preserve and interpret his vision and his doctrine. In addition to his responsibilities as Director of Novices and Director of the motherhouse, Brother Irenee was elected as First Assistant to the Superior General. He served in all three capacities during most the long and influential generalate of Brother Timothy. Thus for almost thirty years, this protege of De La Salle was in the best possible position to influence the direction that the Institute would take and to maintain continuity with the spirit and ideals of the Founder that he first encountered at Parmenie.

As Director of Novices during this long period, Brother Irenee was a major influence on all the young candidates entering the Institute in the first half of the eighteenth century. He could make vivid for them his own personal recollections of John Baptist de La Salle. He was most strict in enforcing both in his young charges, and in himself first of all, an exact and literal observance of every detail of the Common Rule. He inculcated in his novices a special devotion to the Blessed Virgin since she had been such an important focus of his own devotional practice from his childhood at his mother's knee all through the crises of his troubled life. He was particularly devoted to the Immaculate Conception. He formed a confraternity of boarding students at Saint Yon under that title and had Mary Immaculate enshrined in the motherhouse as its first superior.

The personal spirituality of Brother Irenee was characterized, as it was in his spiritual father, by continual attention to the presence of God and by the most austere practices of mortification and personal penance. It was his custom to inflict on his own flesh the severest torments in the hope of winning from divine Providence the forgiveness of his own sins, more vocations for the Institute, and the perseverance of his novices. In his last will and testament, he asked to be buried in the brown robe of a serving Brother and that all the prayers and masses that might be said for him after his death, as well as whatever merits might be due to his good works during life, be applied to the souls in purgatory.

As Assistant to the Superior General, Brother Irenee seems to have been a conservative force in the administration of the Society. Thus he took an active part in preserving and publishing the writings of De La Salle, especially the *Meditations,* the *Collection,* and the *Method of Mental Prayer.* In chapters and administrative councils he opposed the opening of new schools or the development of new institutional forms such as boarding schools and teacher training colleges. He was fearful, not only that the resources of the Institute would be spread too thin, but also that the time and energy required for such apostolic works might begin to interfere with the schedule of spiritual exercises. When commissioned by the Superior General to visit the communities, he seems to have encouraged the Brothers, most of them his former novices, to regard the spiritual experience of their novitiate days, isolated from the distractions of apostolic work, as something of an ideal to which they should return.

At this historical distance, it is possible to raise some questions as to whether the influence of Brother Irenee was always for the best. Having met the Founder in a contemplative setting far removed from the Brothers and their apostolic ministry, having himself been a failure in mastering the elementary principles of classroom management, having been engaged for most of his life in the isolation of the novitiate and motherhouse, it could be argued that he had a one-sided view of the Founder's charism and the finality of the Institute. All of this may have served to overemphasize the contemplative and monastic elements in the spirituality that would be proposed to the Brothers in the Institute, to dichotomize their spiritual life from their apostolic work, to obscure the sort of apostolic spirituality that can be found, for example, in many of De La Salle's writings and especially in the *Meditations for the Time of Retreat.*

There is only one further matter needed to complete the story and that concerns the eventual reconciliation of Claude Francois Dulac de Montisambert, become Brother Irenee, with the surviving members of his family. It may be recalled that in his long journey that led to Parmenie, the principal reason why the young pilgrim was refused entrance into one monastery after another was his inability to obtain the consent of his father. Once Claude resigned his commission in the army, he had determined to live apart and unknown to the world, his family and friends. This was an important factor also in his decision to enter the Institute of De La Salle. However, after some years spent with the Brothers at Saint Yon, he began to have scruples about whether or not all of his old gambling debts, considered to be debts of honor, had been settled by his father. He asked Brother Timothy, the Superior General, to make discreet inquiries about this matter the next time the affairs of the Institute would bring him to the vicinity of Orleans. He stipulated, however, that Brother Timothy was in no way to betray his own whereabouts or his present situation.

Near frantic excitement overcame the household at Montisambert when it was learned that Claude, long since thought dead, was still alive. In response to his inquiries, Brother Timothy learned that both the father and Alphonse, the older brother and regimental captain, had died some years before. Moved by the tears and entreaties of the mother, Brother Timothy could hold the secret no longer. The mother, unable to travel, made the initial contact with her son by letter and through a friend of the family in Rouen. Still wishing to remain unknown to the world, Brother Irenee was at first reluctant to continue the correspondence. Eventually Brother Timothy had to order his Assistant to grant the last wish of his dying mother and to visit her at Montisambert.

Brother Irenee died at Saint Yon in 1747. Shortly before his death, on the pretext of hiring an artist to retouch a painting of the Founder, Brother Timothy managed to have a portrait painted of his saintly Assistant. In some respects Brother Irenee bore a striking resemblance to John Baptist de La Salle. Indeed there are those who think that the so-called "Rue de Sevres" portrait of the Founder, discovered in the 1950's and since widely circulated among the Brothers, is actually that of Brother Irenee.

As the youngest of those involved in the encounters at Parmenie, Brother Irenee was the last to go to his heavenly reward. Only the hermitage remains at Parmenie to bear silent witness to the drama that took place there. It is time, then, to return to Parmenie to trace, however, briefly, the subsequent history of that holy hill forever sanctified by the memory of Louise, De La Salle and Montisambert.

EPILOGUE

The History of Parmenie After Sister Louise

This epilogue is a summary of the last three chapters of Leo Burkhard's Parménie. *Prepared by Luke Salm, it was reviewed and approved by the author. The final paragraph is an update on the present situation at Parmenie and the prospects for its future.*

After the death of Sister Louise in 1727, Father Soland, her choice as chaplain, continued to serve as director at Parmenie for a number of years. Among the many chaplains who succeeded him during the eighteenth century, two are of special importance. The first was Father Berson de Ponceau who directed the retreats from 1734 to 1743. It was he who presided at the funerals of the last companions of Sister Louise. He also collected and preserved much of the material that would serve as the basis for her later biographies. The other chaplain worthy of note was the Canon Gras du Villard who directed the retreats from 1750 to 1769. Not only did he publish a biography of Sister Louise in 1752 but he also devoted a considerable part of his personal fortune to the restoration of the buildings at Parmenie that had deteriorated badly. After his resignation in 1769, a variety of chaplains, with varying degrees of interest in the place, directed the retreats at Parmenie during the twenty years that remained before the French Revolution.

During the French Revolution, Parmenie was confiscated and put up for sale. The last chaplain prior to the Revolution, Father Marion, fled to Lyon where he was harbored by a man named Claude Dubia. Once he had taken the civil oath of the clergy, "Citizen Marion" was able to buy back the property at Parmenie for a small sum. At first he was very prudent and kept a low profile, conscious always that the police were watching. Then there came to Parmenie two women, Nanon Bonneton known as "Mother Nanon" and also as "the Saint" together with her sixteen-year-old companion whom she called "Sister Therese." Father Marion was overawed by these women and took them in, but in another sense he was taken in by them. Mother Nanon would go through the countryside selling her ointments, charms and nostrums in a strange mix of medicine, sorcery and religion. Since the fury of the Revolution had died down, Father Marion meanwhile resumed his ministry and crowds of pilgrims began to come again to Parmenie.

The local police, however, soon became suspicious of some of the strange goings on and managed to put the "Holy Mother" in jail for a time. Upon her release she was looked upon as a martyr, telling of visions that she had of the Holy Spirit while she was in jail. She predicted that a new messiah would appear on Mount Parmenie and that a prophet would soon arrive as his precursor. Very conveniently, the "prophet" did appear, none other than Claude Dubia in the guise of the prophet Elias. The thrust of his message was that the world was about to be destroyed by fire, and that only Parmenie would be spared. For those who wanted to escape the terrible deluge of fire, reserved places on the hill were put up for sale at a considerable price; to add to the excitement and expectation, bizarre cultic practices were introduced to prepare for the coming catastrophe. Once more the police intervened and arrested Dubia. The two women fled, Dubia was condemned, fined and jailed in 1829 and eventually died in poverty. The heirs of Father Marion and his sister, who had been wheedled into turning over the title of the property at Parmenie to Dubia, were happy to accept a monetary settlement and Parmenie itself reverted to the custody of the notary of the nearby town of Izeaux.

While the "Prophet Elias" was still in jail awaiting his "messiah," a worthy successor to Sister Louise appeared on the scene in the person of Rosalie Dupont, "Sister Rosalie" as she came to be called. She too was a poor shepherd girl, devout, dedicated and determined. She too had a love for the beautiful hill that had suffered so much both from the orgies of Dubia and his cultists and from the constant struggles for control among the local pastors. At her persuasion the bishop of Grenoble bought the property and appointed a chaplain to minister to the pilgrims and to conduct retreats. The introduction in Rome of the cause of Beatrice d'Ornacieu and the exhumation of her remains at Parmenie gave a new prominence to the place. Responsibility for the shrine was entrusted at first to the Franciscans and then to the Oblates of Mary Immaculate. Disputes arose over the reception of the pilgrims and the sale of religious articles and for a time Sister Rosalie was forced to leave the hill. With the arrival in 1855 of the "white" Benedictines of Mount Olivet, known as the Olivetines, peace was restored. Rosalie was allowed to return to Parmenie where she lived with her nephew Francis Martin and his wife in a guest house near the monastery. She died in 1873. Large crowds attended her funeral and for a long time her grave at Parmenie rivaled those of Blessed Beatrice and Sister Louise as a place of pilgrimage.

The history of Parmenie in the last century is one long series of destructions and desecrations. Bands of treasure hunters regularly looted the place, attracted by rumors of buried treasure there, whether the supposed riches of the Chartreuse nuns, or the legendary loot of Baunin the Gravedigger, or the lost fortune of Claude Dubia. Then the anti-clerical movement in French politics resulted in an order to close the chapel from 1880 to 1890, with only two aging Olivetines allowed to remain on the property. The definitive departure of the Olivetines in 1903 only increased the incidence of destruction and deterioration. After World War I, a Benedictine monk, the former Count de Malherbe, used some of his personal fortune to restore the shrine which was then officially reopened in 1927. During World War II, Parmenie served as a hideout and meeting place for the resistance movement until the Germans set fire to it in January 1944. The conflagration lasted for two full days. Even after the war, Parmenie had to suffer yet another profanation when a band of strangers settled in, apparently engaged once again in the futile search for buried treasure. In the process, many of the centuries-old tombs that had survived all earlier attacks were despoiled.

In the spring of 1957 Brother Leo Burkhard, a young Christian Brother who had been sent by his superiors in the United States to the Dauphiny country to teach languages in a Brothers' missionary school, came to the ruins of Parmenie for the first time. It was a moving experience for him since he had some years earlier written a biography of John Baptist de La Salle in popular style for English speaking audiences. In this book, entitled *Master of Mischief Makers,* Brother Leo had described his imagined arrival in this spot ten years before he ever set foot in France. Something of the spirit that had energized Sister Louise and Sister Rosalie seems to have taken hold of the young Brother, a spirit rendered more powerful by his knowledge of De La Salle and a personal commitment to the spirit of the Founder and his Institute. Brother Leo was convinced that but for the encounters at Parmenie the Institute might never have survived the crisis of 1714.

Awareness of the past and dreams of the future soon turned into action. Aided by the nephew of the last Benedictine prior at Parmenie, with the support of many former students of the Brothers, a society was formed to establish a center at Parmenie that would do honor to the memory of De La Salle. So it was that in 1964, just 250 years after the sojourn of their Founder, the Brothers of the Christian Schools acquired title to the property.

The work of restoration was barely begun when, in May 1965, a group of arsonists, in an apparent attempt to scare away Brother Leo and to impede the rebirth of Parmenie, set fire to the only shelter left standing on the property. This criminal attack had the opposite effect. Volunteers came from near and far to aid Brother Leo in the laborious manual work involved in the restoration. The ancient glacial rock provided a solid foundation for the new buildings designed to house the chaplain and several Christian Brothers. The chapel was restored and redecorated, many of the original furnishings were recovered from houses and churches in the neighborhood, the relics of Blessed Beatrice were enshrined once more, the crypt grave of Sister Louise in the nave of the chapel was identified and marked with a new marble slab. In addition, a relic of Saint John Baptist de La Salle was obtained from the motherhouse of the Brothers and prominently displayed.

Up until the present the hermitage at Parmenie, although owned by the Institute of the Brothers, has been maintained and financed by a group know as *Les Amis de Parménie,* while Brother Leo Burkhard has been serving as its director. At this writing, however, the future of Parmenie is taking on a new and bright aspect, quite in line with the aspirations of its renovators. Originally under the direct control of the superiors in the motherhouse of the Brothers in Rome, responsibility for the Parmenie property is gradually being turned over to the Brothers of France. Various proposals are being examined to use the property in a way that will better reflect its Lasallian character.

In the summer of 1980, during the celebration marking the tercentenary of the foundation of the Institute by John Baptist de La Salle, Parmenie was the focus of an extraordinary sound and light (*son et lumiére*) festival-pageant during which more than two hundred actors retraced its history down through the centuries. It was also the scene of an impressive gathering of young people from four different continents. The momentum from this religious event has opened up new perspectives for its future use.

Meanwhile, Brother Leo continues to supervise the hermitage with the enthusiasm and dedication that has characterized his relation to this holy place that he first came upon just twenty-five years ago. It has always been his hope that Parmenie will stand for years to come as a worthy memorial to the sainted personages who were its greatest glory: Saint John Baptist de La Salle, his saintly protege Brother Irenee, Blessed Beatrice d'Ornacieux, and the humble shepherdess, Sister Louise.